Pedagogy o.

Series in Critical Narrative

Donaldo Macedo, Series Editor

University of Massachusetts Boston

Now in Print

The Hegemony of English
  by Donaldo Macedo, Bessie Dendrinos, and Panayota Gounari (2003)
Letters from Lexington: Reflections on Propaganda
  New Updated Edition
  by Noam Chomsky (2004)
Pedagogy of Indignation
  by Paulo Freire (2004)
Howard Zinn on Democratic Education
  by Howard Zinn, with Donaldo Macedo (2005)
How Children Learn: Getting Beyond the Deficit Myth
  by Terese Fayden (2005)
The Globalization of Racism
  edited by Donaldo Macedo and Panayota Gounari (2006)
Daring to Dream: Toward a Pedagogy of the Unfinished
  by Paulo Freire (2007)
Class in Culture
  by Teresa L. Ebert and Mas'ud Zavarzadeh (2008)
Dear Paulo: Letters from Those Who Dare Teach
  by Sonia Nieto (2008)
Uncommon Sense from the Writings of Howard Zinn (2008)
Paulo Freire and the Curriculum
  by Georgios Grollios (2009)
*Freedom at Work: Language, Professional, and Intellectual Development in
Schools*
  by María E. Torres-Guzmán with Ruth Swinney (2009)
*The Latinization of U.S. Schools: Successful Teaching and Learning in Shifting
Cultural Contexts*
  by Jason G. Irizarry (2011)
*Culture and Power in the Classroom: Educational Foundations for the Schooling
of Bicultural Students*
  by Antonia Darder (2011)
Changing Lives: Working with Literature in an Alternative Sentencing Program
  by Taylor Stoehr (2013)
Seeds of Freedom: Liberating Education in Guatemala
  by Clark Taylor (2013)
Pedagogy of Commitment
  by Paulo Freire (2014)

PEDAGOGY OF COMMITMENT

Paulo Freire

Translated by
David Brookshaw
and
Alexandre K. Oliveira

Paradigm Publishers
Boulder • London

Copyright © 2014 by Paradigm Publishers

Published in the United States by Paradigm Publishers, 5589 Arapahoe Avenue, Boulder, CO 80303 USA.

Paradigm Publishers is the trade name of Birkenkamp & Company, LLC, Dean Birkenkamp, President and Publisher.

Library of Congress Cataloging-in-Publication Data
Freire, Paulo, 1921–1997, author.
  Pedagogy of commitment : Paulo Freire.
    p. cm.
  ISBN 978-1-59451-972-7 (hc. : alk. paper)
  ISBN 978-1-61205-349-3 (lib. ebook)
  1. Critical pedagogy. I. Title.
  LC196.F455 2014
  370.115—dc23

                                                            2013046451

Printed and bound in the United States of America on acid-free paper that meets the standards of the American National Standard for Permanence of Paper for Printed Library Materials.

Designed and Typeset in New Baskerville by Straight Creek Bookmakers.

18 17 16 15 14   1 2 3 4 5

To those dear friends of mine, who came to me from Paulo and who fought so hard, with him and like him, with honor, seriousness, and lovingness, for a true popular education: Jesús Javier, Gómes Alonso–Pato, José Carlos Barreto, and Carlos Nuñez Hurtado. I acknowledge them and miss them.

Nita
Ana Maria Araújo Freire

Contents

Foreword

When my great friend Roberto Iglesias–a most dear and admired friend of Paulo's–proposed to me the organization of a book with the works that marked my husband's presence in San Luís during the celebrations of his being awarded a doctorate honoris causa degree, as well as in events that followed those, I responded to him with conviction: *yes!*

Tato Iglesias, as he is known–a man, like Paulo, loving and committed to the exploited and the oppressed–invited, then, his peers from the University of San Luís, in Argentina, where he teaches, to publish the records of that moment together. Thus, the book *The Gentle Scream* came into being in 2003.

The book is small in its size, but dense and serious, as it must be as a work by and around Paulo Freire and organized by the creator of the "Universidad Trashumante," whose goal is to take the right word, a commitment to social change, and liberating aid, to the oppressed men and women of Argentina.

In the past few years, some Brazilian men and women who had been familiar with this work in the Spanish language had begun to ask me, "Why not translate it to Portuguese?" I, then, started to ask myself that same question. I decided, therefore, that it would be important to make known to Brazilian readers those texts by Paulo (and only those) contained in *The Gentle Scream*.

If it already was a small book, it became even smaller after the cuts I made. I was, thus, reluctant to do it, but I did because

I have taken as a greater principle giving voice to Paulo. Therefore, my priority was to allow him to "speak his word," and I "invited in" other voices, through their questions and simple comments that contribute objectively to this publication.

Thus the moment that I had waited for opened up: the opportunity to publish a work by Paulo celebrating his and our Latin Americanness, which, while recognized by many of us, is still a ways away from being critically comprehended as our common historical, cultural, and political nature. There is a need for acknowledgment of that fact by all of us Brazilian men and women, so as to form a stronger alliance of solidarity, commitment, and tolerance among the various cultures of the nations comprising Latin America. By denying Latin American unity, we lose the possibility of living and enriching ourselves in the interculturality within it.

Thus, the mentioned cuts to *The Gentle Scream* acted as a funnel, but at the same time, the work was broadened. It was broadened in its geographical reach–works done by Paulo in Chile, Paraguay, and Uruguay, in addition to those in Argentina, plus one more piece especially written for the people of Nicaragua. It also more markedly highlighted a topic that was most dear to Paulo: popular education, as it awakens in all of us, progressive educators, a more political than pedagogical concern. The texts focus on its practice in Latin America.

Paulo's presence in Chile, his only visit there since the barbaric and bloody coup d'état led by the dictator Augusto Pinochet (in power 1973–1990) against the Chilean people, resulted from countless invitations. They came from various institutions, among which I wish to point out the El Canelo de Nos Center–a center for popular education where the Chilean interviews published in this volume took place.

The invitation for Paulo to go to Paraguay and the organization of the seminars, parts of which are included in this publication, and which were fundamentally focused around popular education, were by the Colectivo CEAAL-Py (Council for the Education of Adults in Latin America–Paraguay);

Redicoop (Federation of Cooperatives from the Caribbean and Central America); and Decidamos (Campaign for Citizenly Expression), a nongovernmental organization (NGO) created days after the coup d'état that brought down the dictatorship of General Alfredo Stroessner (in power 1954–1989).

Paulo's trip to Uruguay was an initiative of the CIDC (Center for Research and Cultural Development), during the celebrations of its fifteenth year of operation. The works published here were transcribed from the book–created as part of the celebrations–titled *Paulo Freire: Conversing with Educators.*

After ten years of the Sandinista Revolution, Paulo wrote a manifest with that title, which is included in the book, honoring the Nicaraguan people. The name comes from the guerrilla fighter Augusto César Sandino (1895–1934), leader of the rebellion against the North American military presence in Nicaragua between 1927 and 1933. He was executed by President Anastásio Somoza, who took power and ruled as a dictator for more than forty years. Sandino is a hero in much of Latin America. Somoza was deposed by the FSLN (Sandinista Front for National Liberation) in 1979.

Some of the topics addressed by Paulo Freire come up more than once, as they were discussed at different times and places, and since they have their own specificities, those instances cannot be considered repetitions. They remain, thus, autonomous relative to one another; they were spoken using different angles of approach.

I made a point of preserving the colloquial language in the book for all these selections except for the one written for Nicaragua, by his own hand. The other texts originated from impromptu spoken interviews, speeches, and conference talks given by my husband in the Latin American countries mentioned. By keeping faithful to him, to his peculiar manner of speaking in public, I deliver to his readers, and above all to the men and women in those social movements that are concerned with and practice popular education, an agile book, one that is light and easy to read, but one that contains profound reflection and an unquestionable ethical commitment toward the dispossessed, the exploited, and the oppressed of Latin America.

Pedagogy of commitment: that is what Latin America and popular education means. I regret not having been able to include a greater number of texts spoken by Paulo and related to more countries in Latin America, simply because I do not have them.

Nita
Ana Maria Araújo Freire
São Paulo, April 11, 2008

Preface

The publication of *Pedagogy of Commitment* coincides with numerous events and seminars that are taking place around Latin America and in other parts of the world to commemorate the ten years of Paulo Freire's absence due to his untimely death, and to celebrate the presence and timeliness of his thought. The strong participation in these events for educators belonging to different generations demonstrates that Freire's absence from our midst does not diminish the power of the presence of his ideas and the testimony of coherence that marked his practice as an educator and as a human being.

This collection of texts, which most vividly presents several of Freire's dialogues from his travels throughout Latin America (in this case, mostly through Southern Cone countries), displays one of the essential characteristics of his discourse. It is at the same time heavily historically contextualized and laden with meanings that transcend the moment in which it is spoken. In the selections comprising this volume and dating back to the late '80s and early '90s, Freire clearly positions himself with respect to the perversities of neoliberal thought and what led to the downfall of the socialist experiments of Eastern Europe. At the same time, he reaffirms his convictions, which are not in the least naïve, regarding the political nature of education, its ethical and aesthetic significance, and the meaning of hope as the engine of progressive educators' practice.

The moments captured here also display the ease with which Freire moved among different types of audiences, his strong disposition toward dialogue, and his great capacity for blending methodological rigor with affection for his interlocutors. Having had the opportunity to meet with several of those groups afterward, I was always struck by the reports from participants in those dialogues and how they evoked not only the strength of his ideas, but also the example set by his dialogical disposition and the affection with which he related to the participants on a human level.

The context in which the countries of the Southern Cone lived in the '90s was marked, on one hand, by limited redemocratization processes following lengthy periods of military dictatorship and, on the other, by hegemony of neoliberal policies and thought. Taking that context as a reference, Freire's discourse, on one hand, denounces the immobilistic and fatalistic character of that thought and, on the other, announces the necessity to reaffirm the political nature of education, to revive hope in the possibility of change to that order, and to emphasize education's commitment to processes leading to the radicalization of democracy and the constitution of active citizenship in our societies. In his interventions, he also demonstrates a distancing of himself relative to the socialist experiments of Eastern Europe, above all due to the authoritarian and bureaucratic nature of how they were conducted, and to the dogmatism that marked some of their leadership formulations. At the same time, however, he reaffirms his belief in the dream of building a democratic socialism of historic possibility in our societies. His affirming of his political convictions was always undertaken with profound respect for his adversaries and for the right to differ, within a recurring criticism of sectarianism.

In that context, it is possible to understand the strong identity and influence Paulo Freire exercised in the field of popular education practices in Latin America. Since the early '60s, those practices have come to constitute a significant movement for education and culture, one that has contributed to broadening the re-democratization processes in the continent toward the attainment of societies that are more just and equitable. It has also strengthened the popular sectors as protagonists, through their collective subjects, with special emphasis on social movements.

The creation of the CEAAL (Council for the Education of Adults in Latin America) network in the beginning of the '80s, with Paulo Freire as its first president, led to an association today with approximately 200 affiliated NGOs from twenty-one countries in the continent. It is one of the Latin American spaces where Paulo Freire's propositions continue to be a fundamental reference today in the effort to reinvent popular-education practices and their paradigms, in light of the new challenges inherent to this beginning of a millennium.

One of the most important contributions made by Paulo Freire, and of the popular-education current that found in him its fundamental inspirations, was to develop a view of the educative phenomenon within a farther-encompassing space than that of school, without ever refuting its importance as an educative institution. Freire's reflections on the educational practices within social movements, on diverse forms of sociability and coexistence within popular groups, on actions by political parties, on the practices of government, and on distinct manifestations of popular culture, have lent undeniable consistency to the need to think of education within a greater scope than that of school.

It should be noted, however, that Paulo Freire did not attribute any value judgment or greater relevance to educational practices that take place beyond the school grounds. On the contrary, his writings show great concern with not severing educational practice in his reflections on popular education. That way, he avoided falling into the traps posed by definitions identifying popular education as "nonformal," or as a "parascholastic" practice, and of him as the proponent of a "society without schools."

Freire's discourse was always directed at educators who operate both within schools and in other realms of social practice.

They put us face-to-face with the necessity of understanding popular education as a host of practices and formulations that permeate the different realms of social relations, while recognizing the specificities of the various practices and of the distinct spaces where they develop. The constant reference to his remarkable stint at the Municipal Department of Education in the City of São Paulo, during the Luiza Erundina administration (Workers' Party [PT], 1989–1992), shows the degree of commitment and challenge in that experience. It had as its pedagogical platform the following statement: *Building a democratic and popular public education.* The present growth in the movement for "educator cities" and its clamor for turning all urban spaces and equipment into educational spaces is, today, one expression of that broadened view of educational practice.

At this important moment of a turn toward democracy in Latin America, various civil'society players discuss the need for a process of integration that overcomes the strict limits of the markets and strongly incorporates new citizenship, democracy, and sustainability practices. Popular education is, once again, challenged to play a protagonist role in the building of these new possibilities for change. Without a doubt, Freire's propositions help us a great deal in the building of integrative matrixes for new popular-education practices that can meet the challenges of the new winds blowing, above all, in the Southern Cone of our continent.

More than ever, a *pedagogy of commitment* is needed as the concretization of the transformative hope that fuels the popular-education practices whose starting point is *indignation* before the disastrous consequences of the neoliberal plan. Those practices affirm the possibility of *building dreams*, of more just, equitable societies that are substantively democratic and sustainable.

Pedro Pontual
September 2007

Part I

Argentina

Paulo Freire's Presence at the National University of San Luís

Speech

I Feel Happy and Challenged[1]

My first words, filled with gratitude, are directed at Nélida Esther Picco, the university president; at Germán Arias, dean of the faculty of Human Sciences; and above all, at Professor "Tato" (Roberto Iglesias), whom I learned to like well many years ago, since his stay in São Paulo, when we saw each other almost every day—we talked and worked together. Since then, it has always given me joy to get word from him, as I felt stimulated by his perseverance and his will. We joined together in the dream of changing the world.

First of all, I would like to apologize since it has been some time since I spoke my *Portunhol* [a rule-governed mixture of Portuguese and Spanish], and I am having a little difficulty re-encountering the exercise of a language other than my own. Some think that Spanish is poorly spoken Portuguese, and that Portuguese is poorly spoken Spanish. However, that is not so; they are different languages. I became convinced of that in Chile, when after seeing me teach a class, my younger son said to me, "Wow, Dad, you continue to speak Spanish really badly." And he was right. Nevertheless, now, little by little, I am returning to my *Portunhol*-speaking experience.

How can I thank you all, who have gathered here for this festive occasion of tender friendship and homage? One possibility that I will rule out from the outset is taking advantage of this fraternal gathering to burden you with an academic lecture, to pick up the microphone and speak for an hour and a half about the values of education. That would be terrible, even if academic classes are necessary, fundamental. Were it not for academic conversations, we would not be here.

My position is not one to refute academia, because in some way we are academic. What we are not is academistic. All things have their time and their opportunity, and I believe this is not the time for an academic class, even though this conversation of ours is a serious conversation, as those conversations we had heard previously were serious. Another possibility would be to grab the microphone, say, "Thank you very much; I am flattered," and leave.

That, in addition to being poor manners, would be an aggressive, pretentious, and arrogant attitude that I, obviously, refuse as well. That being the case, I shall prefer to say a few words of thanks, of acknowledgment of what a celebration such as this one means to Nita and myself: a challenge, while a responsibility.

I would also like to say that events such as this fill me with joy. I like that. A person must be ill or a liar to say they feel badly about parties like this. I always say that I consider myself an intensely needy person, and I believe one of my best virtues is this feeling of need, a necessity for the other man, the other woman. I have never felt that I was complete in and of myself. I need others. And that might be why I can understand that others also need me. This celebration, all these people, the words I have heard, all this does not entitle me to arrogance. Quite the opposite, I feel happy and pleased. I would actually say, "May other doctoral degrees come!"

I say that with simplicity and without embarrassment because I feel challenged. The more honors such as this one I receive, the more I feel a duty to be responsible. The honoris causa doctoral degree is not given to just anyone. It is given for a reason. It is necessary to know if it is justified from the standpoint of respect for truth, for history, for science, from the standpoint of ethics. In a world where there is little shame left, it is necessary to know that the university awarding a doctoral degree is not making a mistake. I am convinced that this university is not making an error by honoring me so. I say that because I cannot stand for false modesty. To me, false modesty is worse than immodesty. When I was young, I would listen to orators who would start out saying, "I should not have been the one to receive this award, but rather someone more competent than me." I would always ask myself, "Why doesn't he leave, then? Why did he agree to come?" I understand this party as a call to responsibility. The same way the university acknowledges today what I have been saying and doing for many years, it can just as well symbolically take the doctoral degree away tomorrow, should I betray my past, my present, and recant myself. I seek strength more in the recognition granted me by the university than in myself. I look to you for the strength I need not to betray the principles that caused the University of San Luís to honor me.

When I say, "May other doctoral degrees come," I do so because however many more degrees I shall have, the more humbly responsible I will feel. For all that, I thank you. I am very appreciative of the reference someone made to *Pedagogy of Hope.*[2] I am seventy-five years old, facing some difficulties from the point of view of the body. I am undergoing some sort of separation between mind and body, as if my mind were twenty-five years old, when I know that my body is seventy-five, and can know by anticipation that the body won't be able to follow the mind. You do not know what it means to wish to do something and not to have the means to do it. For example, to work at night: I just about cannot do it any longer.

To sum up, I would like to say that as a political educator, as a man who thinks about the educational practice, I remain profoundly hopeful. I reject immobility, apathy, and silence. I say in my last book, *Pedagogy of Autonomy,*[3] that I am not hopeful on a whim, but rather out of conditioning dictated by my human nature. It is not possible to live fully as a human being without hope. Hold on to hope. Thank you very much!

Notes

All annotations were contributed by Ana Maria Araújo Freire.
1. Speech delivered at the Universidad de San Luís–Argentina, following the award of the doctor honoris causa degree, on August 16, 1996.
2. Editora Paz e Terra, 12th edition (São Paulo, 2005), preface by Leonardo Boff, notes by Ana Maria Araújo Freire.
3. Editora Paz e Terra, 36th edition (São Paulo, 2007). Commemorative edition celebrating the printing of one million copies in September 2007.

Seminars on Critical Pedagogy

Critical Pedagogy Practice[1]

First of all, I would like to thank you for this demonstration of affection, the folks who came from far away and traveled for hours, even while knowing that the time we have available would be scarce. The second thing I would like to thank you for is this silence. It helps me to be able to speak.

This afternoon, we are going to address the topic of "educative practice," and how we have been understanding or trying to comprehend this practice as our commitment to life and the world.

First of all, it is not possible to exercise the educative task without asking ourselves, as male and female educators, what our concept of man and of woman is. All educative practice implies the questioning, "What do I think of myself and of others?" It has been a while, since *Pedagogy of the Oppressed*, that I analyzed what I then termed the quest for Being More. In that book, I defined man and woman as historical beings that make and remake themselves socially. And that social experience ultimately makes us, constitutes us, as we are being. I would like to insist on this point: men and women, while historical beings, are incomplete, unfinished, unconcluded beings. This nonconclusion of being is not, however, restricted to the human species. It reaches every vital species. The world of life is a permanently unfinished world in motion. Nevertheless, at a given moment in our historical experience, we, women and men, manage to make our existence into something more than just living. In a certain sense, men and women invent what we call human existence: we got ourselves up on our feet, freed our hands, and that freeing of our hands is, in large part, responsible for what we are.

The invention of ourselves as men and women was made possible by the fact that we freed our hands to use them for other things. We do not have a date for this event, which is lost in the depths of history. We did this wonderful thing that was the invention of society and the development of language. And it was then, at that precise moment, in the midst of that and other "leaps" we accomplished, that we, women and men, attained this formidable moment, the realization that we are unfinished, unconcluded, incomplete. The trees and the other animals are also incomplete, even though they do not know themselves as incomplete. Human beings are at an advantage in that: we know we are unfinished. It is precisely there, in this radical form of human experience, in which the possibility of education resides. Conscious awareness of our incompleteness created what we call the "educability of being." Education is, thus, a human specificity.

Our self-aware unfinishedness is what will allow us to notice the *non-I*. The world is the first *non-I*. You, for example, are a *non-I* to me. It is the presence of the natural world as a *non-I* that will act as a stimulus to develop the *I*. And in that sense, it is awareness of the world that creates my awareness. I come to know what is different from me, and in that act, I come to know myself. Obviously, the relationships that start to become established between the *we* and *objective reality* opened up a host of question marks, and those questions led to a search, the intent to comprehend the world and to comprehend our position within it. It is in that sense that I use the expression *reading of the world* as preceding the *reading of the word*. Many centuries before knowing how to read and write, men and women had been intellectualizing the world, taking it in, understanding it, reading it. This capacity for taking in the objectiveness of the world stems from a characteristic of the vital experience that we call curiosity.

Were it not for curiosity, for example, we would not be here today. Curiosity is, alongside conscious awareness of incompleteness, the essential engine of discovery, knowledge. Were it not for curiosity, we would not learn. Curiosity pushes us forward, motivates us; it causes us to unveil reality through action. Curiosity and action enter into a relationship to produce different moments or levels of curiosity. What I am trying to say is that at a given moment, pushed on by their own curiosity, man and woman in process, under development, come to recognize themselves as unfinished, and the first consequence of that is that the being that feels unfinished goes into a permanent process of searching. I am unfinished, and so is a tree, but I am more unfinished than a tree because I know I am. As an almost unavoidable consequence of knowing I am unfinished, I insert myself in a constant movement of searching, not in a punctual search for this or that, but rather an absolute search, which could lead to the very search for my origin, which might lead to a search for the transcendental, to a religious search that is as legitimate as a nonreligious search. If there is something that goes against the nature of human beings, it is the nonsearch and, thus, immobility. When I say immobility, I am referring to that which exists within mobility. A person can be profoundly mobile and dynamic even while being physically immobile or static. Therefore, when I speak about this, I am not referring to physical mobility or immobility; I am speaking about an intellectual search, about my curiosity around something, about the fact that I can seek even if I may not find. For example, I may spend my life in searches that apparently do not result in much, and all the while, the fact that I am in search results fundamentally from my nature as a researcher, being in search of something.

Now, there cannot be search without hope, and that is so because a condition for this human search is that it is undertaken with hope. For that reason, I maintain that men and women are hopeful not due to being obstinate, but rather because they are beings that are always searching. That is the human condition for searching: doing it with hope. Searching and hope make up part of human nature. Searching without hope would be a tremendous contradiction. For this reason, your presence in the world, and mine, is the presence of someone who moves along, and not of someone who is simply there. And it is not possible to move along without hope of arriving. Therefore, it is impossible to find a human being devoid of hope. What we can indeed conceive of are moments of hopelessness. During the process of the search, there are moments when we detain ourselves and say to ourselves, "There is nothing to be done." That is understandable; I can understand that one might come down to that position. What I cannot share is the notion that one should remain in that position. It would be like a betrayal of our very nature, our hopeful and disquietedly searchful nature.

These reflections we are engaging in aim to signal essential issues to our educative practice. How can I educate without being involved in a critical understanding of my own search and without respecting the students'? This has to do with the dailiness of our educative practice as men and women. I always say "men and women" because I learned many years ago, while working with women, that it is immoral to say only "men." That is what ideology is all about! From the time I was a boy, in school, I learned something else: I learned that when we say "man," that includes women as well. I learned that in grammar, the masculine gender prevails. That is to say that if all the people gathered here were women, but if one single man were to turn up, I would have to say "*todos*" [masculine "all"], not "*todas*" [feminine "all"], when referring to all of you. What seems to be a matter of grammar is obviously not. It is ideology, and it took me a long time to understand it. I had already written *Pedagogy of the Oppressed*. Read the early editions of that book, and you will see that it was written in sexist language. North American women made me see that I had been deformed by sexist ideology.

Getting back to our topic: it is impossible, except for when one falls into hopelessness, to stop searching and, therefore, to stop having hope. I was telling you that another fundamental issue pertaining to educative practice is nonconclusion, given that it is within his/her nonconclusion that it becomes possible for a human being to be educated. Every learner, every teacher, discovers him-/herself as a curious being, as a seeker, a researcher, an inquirer, an unfinished being—thus, capable of picking up on and getting across the meaning of reality. It is in this very process of developing intelligence on reality that communication on what was apprehended becomes possible. For example, at the very moment when I understand, when I can reason about, how a microphone works, I will be able to communicate about it, to explain it. Comprehension implies the ability to pass it on. In more academic language I would say intelligibility subsumes the communicability of its object.

One of the most beautiful and gratifying tasks we have as teachers is to help learners constitute an intelligibility of things, to help them learn to comprehend and to communicate that comprehension to others. That allows us to attempt a theory of the intelligibility of objects. That does not mean this is an easy task. A teacher does not have the right to engage in an incomprehensible sort of discourse in the name of academic theory and then say, "They should handle it!" Nevertheless, he or she should not make cheap concessions, either. His or her task is not to create simplism, because simplism is disrespectful to the learners. The simplistic teacher believes that the learners will never rise up to being able to understand him or her and, thus, reduces the truth to a half truth; that is, a false truth. The duty of educators is not to fall into simplism, because simplism hides the truth, but rather to be simple. What we have to do is adopt a simplicity that does not minimize the seriousness of our object of study, but rather highlights it.

Simplicity makes for the intelligibility of the world, and that intelligibility of the world brings within it the ability to communicate it. It is thanks to that possibility that we are social, cultural, historic, and communicative beings. For this reason, a breakaway from a dialogic relationship is not only the violation of a democratic principle, but also a violation of human nature itself. Democratic teachers intervene in the world through the cultivation of curiosity and of hopeful intelligence, which unfolds into a communicating comprehension of the world. And we do that in different ways. We intervene in the world through our concrete practice; we intervene in the world through responsibility, through an aesthetic intervention, every time we are able to express the beauty of the world.

When early humans drew images of animals on rocks, they were already intervening aesthetically upon the world, and since they surely already made moral decisions, they were also intervening in an ethical sense. Precisely to the extent that we become able to intervene, able to change the world, to transform it, to make it more beautiful or uglier, we become ethical beings. To date, it has never been known, for example, that a group of African lions had thrown bombs over the cities of Asian lions. We have not to date learned of the existence of some lion that had killed in premeditated fashion. It is we, humans, who have the possibility of taking up an ethical position, who do those types of things. We are the ones who kill and assassinate men like Mauricio López,² whom I knew and whose absence I feel deeply, for whom I have great respect and admiration, and whom I miss. It was not elephants that made Mauricio and so many others vanish; it was the men of this country who probably acted with the complicity of some gringo presence. Only beings who have reached the possibility of being ethical become able to betray ethics. The fundamental task for educators is to live ethically, to practice ethics on a daily basis both with children and with youths. That is much more important than the subject of biology, if one is a biology teacher.

What matters is the testimony we provide through our conduct. Inevitably, each class and every bit of conduct is testimony to the manner, ethical or not, in which one faces life. How do

I work in the classroom? How do I work, with my students, through the issue of nonconclusion, of curiosity? How do I work the problem of hope interspersed with hopelessness? What should I do? Should I cross my arms? Should I lunge into some sort of blind struggle with no way out? We must educate through example, without thinking, for that reason, that we are going to save the world. What harm could it do me, or you all, to think, for example, that I came into the world with the mission to save you? It would be disastrous. I am a man like all of you, and like you, I have a job to do, and that is enough already. The world gets saved if we all, in political terms, fight to save it.

There is something in the air in Argentina, in Brazil, all over the world, that threatens us. That something is the ideology of immobility and fatalism, according to which we have nothing left to do, according to which reality is immutable. I am tired of hearing sentences like this: "It is terrible; in Brazil there are thirty million women, men, and children starving to death, but what can we do; that is reality." I am tired of hearing that the unemployment that is spreading around the world is a fatality of the end of the century. Neither hunger nor unemployment are fatalities; not in Brazil, not in Argentina, not anywhere. I ask the fatalist, in a book that I am writing now, Why must it be that agrarian reform is not a fatality as well in Brazil? You have heard about the speculative world of dollars, millions of dollars traveling around daily through the computers of the world, from place to place, looking for the highest return, have you not? That, to them, is not a fatality either. It is necessary, says the neoliberal leadership, to discipline those speculative flows so as to avoid crises. It would seem that this sort of thing can indeed be done. Why might it be that, when the interests of the dominant classes find themselves compromised, there is no fatalism? Nevertheless, it always comes across as fatalism, as if through the art of magic, every time the popular classes are compromised.

One of the great challenges we must face up to today is this confrontation with that immobilistic and fatalistic ideology.

There is no immobility in history. There is always something that we can do or redo. A lot is being said about globalization. You must have noticed that globalization comes through as some sort of abstract entity that gave rise to itself out of nothing and against which we can do nothing. Globalization it is, end of story! That is a very different question. Globalization simply represents a given moment in the development process of a capitalist economy that got to this stage owing to a given political orientation that is not necessarily the only one.

With what I have said thus far, I sought to address the topic of how I see teaching practice in light of the current historic reality. I have told you that there is no teaching practice devoid of curiosity, without unfinishedness, without being capable of intervening in reality, without being capable of being the makers of history, while at the same time being made by it.

I have also told you that one of the fundamental tasks, both here and in Brazil and around the world, is to develop a critical pedagogy. And I tell you this not as someone who already "has been"; I tell you this as someone who "is being." Just like all other people, I too am being, in spite of my age. As a function of and in response to our own human condition, as conscious, curious, and critical beings, the educator's practice consists of fighting for a critical pedagogy that can give us tools to assert ourselves as the subjects of history. Such a practice must be based on solidarity. Maybe never before as we do at this moment have we needed the significance and practice of solidarity more.

In closing, I would like to reiterate: I continue on with the same hope, with the same desire to fight as when I started. I resist the word *old*. I do not feel old. I feel that I have been helpful, full of hope, and eager to fight.

Elements of the Educative Situation[3]

I thank you for your understanding. It is not just the work; it is the emotion, the frayed emotion. It is not just this meeting with you; it is the memory. It is not because of what I did yesterday; it is because of what I did before yesterday, what I did last month; it is the sum of my days that is tiring me. It is not simply a matter of pushing a button and getting memory to work. . . .

I am glad to realize that you have been comprehending me. If I could, today, I would stay all day.

Now, as suggested by Roberto Iglesias, I will try to say a few things that you probably already know, or can guess, on the topic of education and teacher education.

I would like to start with an intellectual exercise: that of thinking about the situation we call the *educative situation.* An educative situation is not just any situation. The situation of a luncheon, for example, may contain in itself a few educative moments, but it is not necessarily an educative situation. We could think of an educative situation at home, in the relationship between a father, a mother, and their children. However, I would rather think about the typical educative situation, between teachers and students. It does not matter at what school it might be, elementary, secondary, university-level, or culture circle. What I would like to do is analyze and "discover" with you what the constitutive elements of the educative situation are.

Let us imagine that we are in a classroom, where teacher and students are. What is the teacher's task? In simple terms, we might say that the teacher's task is to teach, and the students' task is to learn.

We see, then, that the first constitutive element of the educating situation is the presence of a subject, the educator, who has a specific task; that is, to educate.

The educative situation also implies the presence of learners, students, and the second element of the educative situation.

What else do we discover in the practice of that experience? In the first place, we discover that the presence of the educator and learners does not take place in the air. The educator and learners meet at a certain space. That space is the pedagogical space, to which teachers oftentimes neglect giving due consideration. If we were to detain ourselves in an analysis of how important the pedagogical space is, we would spend the whole morning in discussions. We might focus, for example, on the legal impediments stemming from the public authorities' disrespect toward those spaces. Even though there are differences from space to space, different places, this is almost a historic tradition in Latin America.

When I was invited, in 1989, to take office as head of public education for the City of São Paulo, the municipal public-school system had 675 schools, about one million students, and 35,000 teachers. Sixty percent of the 675 schools were in full process of material deterioration. Many, in the information age, didn't even have chalk. In many schools, the restrooms were absolutely unusable. It was an adventure to walk into a restroom. Schools lacked food, supplies....

The material conditions in the spaces themselves may or may not be pedagogical. How can a teacher, no matter how diligent she might be, how disciplined and careful she might be, ask her students not to litter the classroom, not to break the chairs, not to write on their desks, when the very government that should set an example does not show a modicum of respect for those spaces? The more the school's administration, the local education authorities, and the different centers of power demonstrate to the children and their families their zeal and care toward the school, by repairing ceilings and walls, by delivering chalk and plants and trees, the more that demonstration of respect will educate the children.

I was told, and I don't know whether it is true, that the management of the São Paulo subway system has a department in charge of taking damaged cars and broken seats out of circulation daily. This department removes the trains, repairs them, and returns them to service immediately, so that the cars are always clean and undamaged. This repairing of damaged equipment inhibits the seat-breaker. There is an indubitable relationship between our material conditions and our mental, spiritual, ethical condition.

The third element of the educative situation is, then, the pedagogical space. And since there is no space without time, then pedagogical time is another constitutive element of the educative situation. Regrettably, we educators don't often ask ourselves, "What do I do with my pedagogical time? How can I use it more effectively?" We almost never ask ourselves, "At whose service, and of what things, is pedagogical time?" We are dealing here with fundamental questions. Obviously, educative time is at the service of knowledge production. And since there is no knowledge production that is not directly linked or associated with ideals, the first question we must ask is, "At whose service, and at the service of what ideals, do we, together with the students, produce knowledge within the school's time-space?" And when one goes over this point, one discovers that the pedagogical time-space is used, above all, against the interests of the poor children, even if not exclusively against them.

Let us propose that the children get to school at 8 o'clock. At 8:15, the bell rings, and the children line up "military style." A few teachers have not yet arrived. Regrettably, that goes on. By 8:20, the children are getting to their classrooms. The teacher takes attendance, and there go another ten minutes. It is now 8:30, and the teacher—in this caricature I am painting—if he/she is tired, won't do anything important, for he/she is thinking that the midmorning snacks will be served at 10 o'clock. At that time, the bell rings, and the children rush out yelling, while the teachers gather in the "teachers' room" rather than going out to observe the students during recess. They fail to participate in this extremely rich pedagogical moment; that is, the moment when the children are letting out their fears, their anger, their anxieties, their joy, their sadness, and their desires. The children are pouring their souls out at recess, and the teachers remain in the "teachers' room," oblivious to that essential human experience! After recess, the children have their milk, and there go minimally another thirty minutes, not to mention other bits of dead time. By the end of the day, the children had, out of a four-hour pedagogical span, two and a half or three hours of class. They have lost at least one hour. That lost hour represents one hour of learning that did not take place. The worst part is that no one even discussed that loss of knowledge-production time; after all, should we have done so, we would have learned something, at least. Unfortunately, the school experience falls into a daily routine, which is not thought about, but just lived out. This is a pending sort of reflection that is rarely undertaken in universities. And I say that with sadness. As teachers, we have an obligation to know, debate, and analyze such things.

We have seen, thus far, that there cannot be an educative situation without the figure of the teacher and that of the students, both of whom meet at a given space along the course of a given teaching time. However, there is something more that is essential to the educative situation. That something more is the curricular content, the programmatic elements of the school, which I, as teacher, have the obligation to teach, and the students have the obligation to learn. In more academic language, in knowledge theory, those content items are termed the *cognoscible objects*, and the young men and women who seek an education toward becoming teachers must know them. I put out those concepts because I believe that, even within the practice of popular education, the people have the right to gain command of academic language.

I mention this because there are popular educators who feel that, in the name of the revolution, it is correct to break away from academia. The way I see it, that is an error; it is a betrayal of the people. The right thing to do is to exchange with academia, not to turn one's back to it. Our issue is not to be against academia, but rather to remake it, place it at the service of the interests of most people. We must lend prestige to academia; that is, place it at the service of the people. Ever since men and women invented life in society, cognoscible objects have been noticed and studied through the exercise of curiosity. The people have the right to know, need to know, that items of school content are called *cognoscible objects*—that is, objects that can become known.

And, here, another important topic comes up. Cognoscible objects are noticed through the exercise of curiosity. Therefore, as teachers, we must take great care in preserving the curiosity of children. How many times have you observed, perhaps at a friend's home, a father and mother having a conversation with guests, when a child, maybe a three- or four-year-old, suddenly runs into the room with a question for the father, "Quiet! Can't you see I am talking to someone else? Geez, why must you come in here now with such nonsense?" My goodness! I am not one to throw stones at anyone, or to create feelings of guilt; nevertheless, such conduct is appalling. This is a castrating sort of behavior that curtails one of our most precious possessions, which is curiosity. Without curiosity, we could not even manage to become fathers and mothers. All educative time is a time for questions and answers, a time to discipline and to systematize one's own question.

One afternoon, many years ago, in Recife, the president of the university came to our home to discuss a problem at the university. We were out on the terrace, when suddenly one of my kids, who must have been four or five at the time, came to ask me something. I interrupted the conversation, listened to the boy, answered him, and then said, "Listen; your father is talking to a friend who also has questions to ask and who answers questions, as well. Therefore, if you have another question to ask, why don't you save it in your memory and ask me later? That way, Dad can continue his conversation with his friend." It is necessary to protect the boy's right to ask questions, to satisfy his curiosity. At the same time, however, it is necessary to tell him that there are times for asking questions and times for abstaining, or what we call in ethics *assuming the limits of freedom.* Without limits, there can be no freedom, and there can be no authority either. The formidable question put to us by educators is how to set limits, and what limits really consist of, which among them are those still in need of implementation.

Let us now return to the matter of objects of knowledge. The more we think about what teaching is and what learning is, the more we discover that there cannot be one thing without the other, that those two moments are simultaneous. They complement each other in such a way that one who teaches learns as he/she teaches, and one who learns teaches as he/she learns. It is not for no reason that in French the same verb means to teach and to learn (the verb *apprendre*). The question is how to deal with this apparent contradiction. Right now, in this moment of speaking with you, I am recognizing these things; I am relearning these things, in such a way that you teach me through your process of learning. How so? Through your gazes and your attitudes. An attentive teacher is an alert one who does not only learn from books; who learns in the classroom, who learns from reading people as if they were text. As I speak, as a teacher, I have to develop within myself the critical and affective capacity for reading eyes, the movements of bodies, and the inclination of heads. I must be able to notice if there is someone among us who does not understand what I am saying, and in that case, it is my duty to go over the concept again in a clear manner so as to bring the person back into the process of my discourse. In a sense, you are like a text to me right now, a book I need to read at the same time as I speak. In Brazil, good politicians used to be able to do that, knew how to touch the sensibilities of their listeners. Now with television, that is coming to an end. The practice of teaching goes beyond just walking into a classroom and providing, for example, a classification of nouns. Educative practice is much more than that.

Synthesizing what I have already said about the topic: there isn't, then, a pedagogical situation without a subject who teaches, without a subject who learns, without a space-time within which these relationships take place, and there are no pedagogical situations without objects that can become known. However, the issue does not end here. There is another instance that is constitutive of the educative situation, something that goes beyond the educative situation and, nonetheless, is part of it. There is no educative situation that does not point to objectives lying beyond the classroom, that does not have to do with conceptions, ways of reading the world, aspirations, and utopias. From a technical standpoint, such instance, in philosophy of education, is termed directionality of education. Many people mistake directionality for control, for authoritarianism. Nevertheless, directionality can enable both an authoritarian and a democratic position, the same way that lack of directionality can enable spontaneity.

It is precisely directionality that explains this essential quality of the educative practice that I call the *politicalness of education*. The politicalness of the educative practice is not an invention of subversives, as the reactionary would have it. On the contrary, it is the very nature of the educative practice that leads the educator to be political. As an educator, I am not political because I want to be, but rather because my condition as educator so imposes. That does not mean being supportive of this or that political party, even though I do feel every educator should take a political-party position.

Politicalness is, thus, inherent to the educative practice. That means that, as a teacher, I must have my own and clear political choices, my dreams. After all, what moves us, gives us strength as teachers, if we make so little money, if we are granted so little prestige in this market society? What dream do I have to dream, to discuss with my students? Politicalness reveals two other characteristics of the educative situation. It reveals that, in the educative practice, aesthetics and ethics go hand in hand. The educative practice is beautiful, as is the formation of culture, the development of a free individual. At the same time, such an aesthetic is ethical, for it deals with morality. Hardly ever is a beautiful thing immoral. This puts us in the position to refute the puritanism that is not ethical, is hypocritical, and is a falsification of ethics, of freedom, and of purity.

Recapping, then: there is no educative practice without subjects, without the educator subject and without the learner subject; there is no educative practice outside this space-time that is the pedagogical space-time; there is no educative practice outside the experience of coming to know, what we technically call gnosiologic experience, which is the experience of the process of knowledge production itself; there is no educative practice that is not political; there is no educative practice that is not involved in dreams; there is no educative practice that does not involve values, visions, utopias. There is, thus, no educative practice without ethics.

Education must not fail to take into account all those elements. That is a serious and complex task, and as such, it must be confronted both by those responsible for educative policies and by teachers themselves. We have the responsibility not to try to mold our students, but to challenge them so that they will participate as subjects in their own formative process. The past few days, I have been finishing a new book with old ideas, where I address this topic of teacher education and where I highlight two or three pieces of knowledge, or maxims, that I believe should be part of every teacher's equipment.

One of those maxims, which has long been with me, is one that maintains, "Changing is difficult, but it is possible." What testimony could I provide to the young if my position regarding the world were that of someone convinced that nothing can be done, that nothing can be changed? I would say that in such case, it might be better to leave teaching altogether, and try to make a living some other way. No one can teach classes without having conviction in what they are doing. One cannot say, "I am simply a technician, removed from the world, from history." Not only must I give testimony of my desire for change, but beyond that, I must demonstrate that within me it is more than a belief; it is conviction. If I am not able to give testimony as to my convictions, I lose my ethical base and become a terrible educator because I cannot get across the value of transformation.

Another conviction I consider fundamental is one that maintains, "It is necessary to learn how to listen." There are those who believe that by speaking one learns how to speak, when in reality, it is by listening that one learns how to speak. One cannot speak well who does not know how to listen. And listening always implies not discriminating. How can I comprehend the students from the slums if I am convinced that they are just dirty children who smell? If I am not able to understand that they are dirty because they do not have water to shower with? No one opts for destitution. In Rio de Janeiro, Joãozinho Trinta, an extraordinary man who beautifully organizes Samba Schools during Carnaval, once said something very true: "Only lower-bourgeoisie intellectuals like poverty. The people like beautiful things, luxury." Obviously, the people like well-being, something they do not or cannot have. What we must want is not for the people to remain in poverty, but rather to overcome it. We must fight in order that the people can live well, can have shirts like this one I am wearing, which would have been considered emblematic of the bourgeoisie. We must democratize the good things, not suppress them. I do not reject all things bourgeois, but I do the bourgeois philosophy of life. Some mistakes from the past must be overcome, like thinking that solidarity toward the oppressed is a matter of geography, that it is necessary to leave the more upscale area of town and to go live in poverty in order to show absolute solidarity with them. That does not always work.

Learning how to listen implies not minimizing the other, not ridiculing the other. How can a teacher have good communication with a student having previously devalued or been ironic toward that student? How could a sexist teacher listen to a woman, or a racist one to a black person? I say, if you are a sexist, own up to your sexism, but do not represent yourself as being democratic; you have nothing to do with democracy. At the same time, should you wish to insist on dreams for democracy, you will, then, have to start thinking about overcoming your sexism, classism, and racism.

In the United States, someone just burned black churches, in the first place, as if black men and women did not have souls and, in second place, if admitting that they do have souls, as if the black soul were impure and could mar prayer. It is pitiful that whiteness would give itself the right to be the pedagogue of democracy in the world. The incredible nerve!

Another appropriate conviction for the democratic teacher to hold consists in knowing that to teach is not to transfer content from one's head to the students' heads. To teach is to create the possibility for students, while developing their curiosity and making it more critical, to produce knowledge in cooperation with teachers. The teacher's lot is not to transfer knowledge. The teacher must simply propose to the learners the allocation of the necessary means toward building their own comprehension of their discovery process and of their object of study.

The complexity of the educative practice is such that it faces us with the need to consider all the elements that can lead to a good educative process; it presents the need for the invention of knowledge-creating situations, without which authentic educative practice could not take place. I say this because the virtues and the conditions conducive to good educative practice do not fall from the heavens ready-made. There is no God that sends virtues as presents; there is no divine bureaucracy in charge of giving out virtues. Knowledge and virtues must be created, invented by us. No one is born generous, critical, honorable, or responsible. We are born with those possibilities, yet we must nurse them, develop them, and cultivate them in our daily practices. We are what we are being. The condition for me to be is that I am being. Each one of us is a process and a vision, rather than a destination. It is necessary that I discover, in my own social experience, in my own practice, the path toward better doing what I wish to do. In my teaching practice, I learned the need for coherence, which cannot be a discourse removed from my practice. I learned that I had to seek an almost perfect identification between what I said and what I did. That is the virtue called coherence.

I also discovered that the affective element in my practice was linked to the need to accept the subjectiveness of others, the need not to think that I am the only one in the world who can do certain things, and the need not to resent those who can do things I would like to do but do not do because I am not able to. I found out that I cannot hate anyone who is happy in the world simply because he or she is happy. I also learned that I should continue to inquire as to the difficult situation that creates the unhappiness of others. That respect for the rights of others, that recognition that others can do things that we do not do, is called humility. And humility does not imply a taste for being humiliated. Quite the contrary: the humble person rejects humiliation.

In conclusion, men and women who are teachers, educators, and learners, we must concern ourselves with the creation and re-creation, within ourselves and in our places of work, of those fundamental qualities, the ones that will allow us to realize our dreams.

The Struggle Never Ends, but Is Reinvented: Participants' Questions and Paulo Freire's Answers

How can we motivate students and avoid their becoming adapted to lack of interest, to individualism, and to rampant lack of solidarity?
Keeping our students from settling into apathy is one of our tasks. Obviously, in light of the unemployment problem, it is not easy to motivate people, keep their hopes up. However, it is fundamental that we discuss with learners the very reasons for the being of things, the origins of our difficulties. If we can convince the young that reality, no matter how difficult it is, can be transformed, we will be accomplishing one of the historical tasks of this moment. It must be taken into account that history does not end with every person's individual history. I will be dying in little time, but the history of Brazil goes on with the other Brazilian men and women. History is a process. If we do our part, we will be making a contribution to the following generation. Even if at certain moments one might feel tired, he or she does not have the right to give up on the struggle. What one must have is the right to rest for a day. I do not have the right to give up on the struggle

because I have gotten to be seventy-five years old. I am too young for that.

What is the possible educational utopia in Latin America today?

The possible utopia, not only in Latin America, but also in the world, is the reinvention of societies toward making them more human, less ugly, toward making ugliness into beauty. The possible utopia is to work to make sure our society becomes more visible, more respected all over the world, for all social classes.

Methodologically, how can we organize the resistance?

Starting at our own localities, our sections of town, and our neighborhoods. We need to reinvent the forms of political action. Many people don't even remember who they have voted for. We must value democracy. Not only do we need to know who we have voted for, but also we must know what those men and women we have voted for are doing, request that they be accountable, denounce them if they are not, and not elect them in the following election. We must watch them. Something else that one can do is note the statements by different candidates, their promises made during political campaigning, and then compare and see whether what they said matches up with what they are doing. Generally, during political campaigning, a sort of discourse is upheld that has nothing to do with the practice that follows. We have to make these things public. Denouncing candidates who are not living up to their promises is a form of struggle, a way to break isolation. This is but one example of what can be done.

Is history over? Are the ideologies finished? Are social classes gone?

First of all, we must reject these types of discourse, define them for what they are: purely ideological discourse belonging to a reactionary ideology. History is not over. It continues on alive and beckoning us to fight. Social classes are not gone. They are out there, manifesting their existence in all the streets of the entire world. Exploitation is not gone, and the facts are not irreversible. We must understand that the struggles of the peoples go through different stages, and those stages present different difficulties.

Today I mentioned, on the university radio station, a meeting that took place in Berlin under the impact of the situation in Chiapas, where European scientists put forth a harsh criticism of the neoliberal discourse and practice. It was a very serious analysis that is now going on in Mexico. Gatherings such as that provide testimony that it is possible to fight. It is necessary to fight.

How can we achieve change in teacher attitudes?
In the first place, it is necessary that the teacher be at least inclined toward change. In the second place, the teacher must be clear on what his or her political position is. Education is a political practice, and a teacher, like any other citizen, must make his or her political choice. In the third place, it is necessary that a teacher begin to build his or her coherence, to shorten the distance between his or her discourse and his or her action. How can I adopt a progressive discourse and soon engage in sectarian behavior, filled with race and class prejudice? Such often-veiled contradictions must be exposed. The first struggle the progressive teacher must wage is with him- or herself. That is the beginning of change.

How can we build the pedagogy of mobility?
In the first place, by moving. It is not possible to work toward a pedagogy of movement while remaining static. First, we have to walk, and to walk means, in this case, even if we are sitting, being open to changes and differences. I cannot talk to students about a pedagogy of the world that silences them. If, when faced with a question that creates difficulty, I respond, "Do you know who you are speaking with?," I am closing up the possibility for a pedagogy of mobility. You cannot imagine how much one can learn from the different. Sometimes we do not learn from what's equal, but from what's different

from what we always do. Sometimes we learn even from what's antagonistic. A pedagogy of movement is a pedagogy of openness to others, the different.

When I returned from exile, in one of my first seminars, at the Pontifical Catholic University of São Paulo, I had as a student, a lady of a certain age, certainly a reactionary, who nourished a gratuitous, historical resentment toward my person. When I spoke about what I intended to do, she looked at me and said, "I will not miss one single day of class, Sir, because I want to see if there is coherence between what you say and what you do." I replied, "Very well, thank you very much. I am happy that you will be coming. You will always be well received. I am sure that, when we finish the semester, you will realize, through concrete proof, that what I say coincides with what I do." We never had a close relationship. She was never absent from class, and once the semester was over, she had the highest grade, because she was a serious, studious, intelligent woman. However, she had been reactionary. That was a right she had, to be reactionary, just as I have the right not to be. We courteously said our good-byes, and she said, "Sir, you do what you say!" That was an excellent gift. Actually, the best gift may have been the fact that she came to me, came to see me, and her having said, "I stand converted; now I am a progressive woman." That is not easy! There is always the temptation to reject another who thinks differently.

One must struggle. The teacher who wants to be coherent with respect to his or her democratic and ethical position has the obligation to understand and respect opinions different than his or her own.

How can we resist within unions, in an era when the workers' organizations are devalued and infiltrated by the dominant culture?

This is another very serious issue. In my judgment, the unions should study this current situation with great seriousness. You may have noticed, for example, that strikes have been weakened. Nevertheless, the fact that strikes have lost some of their efficacy does not mean that the struggle should disappear. The struggle is historical. And the manner in which the struggle transpires is also historical, time-space. One does not necessarily wage the struggle the same way here as in Paris.

What is fundamental is to know that the fight isn't over; it never ends, for being historical, it shifts in the manner it presents itself, makes itself. Therefore, it has to be reinvented as a function of the historic and social circumstances. If the teachers' strike produces no results, it is up to educators to scientifically discuss what the most effective form of struggle is at any given moment. The issue is not giving up on the fight, but rather changing the forms of struggle.

With so-called globalization, a multinational company from Chicago that owns a factory in São Paulo, if threatened with a strike, can figure out, in ten minutes, from a computer at that factory, whether it is possible to transfer production to another country, where it may, in fact, be cheaper to operate. They can then shut down the factory in São Paulo, and the strike is over. The issue is not to stop fighting. This is a totalitarian neoliberal discourse.

The issue is changing the way one fights. A new form of struggle must be reinvented, but the struggle must never end.

What would you say to the young people who are discouraged, who never knew their parents' age of struggle?
Young people need to know that human existence is an experience of struggle. It is important to make it clear that struggle, as well as violence, is present throughout human experience. By chiseling away at the rock, a sculptor interrupts the balance of the stone's being. There is a certain creative violence in that.

In the final analysis, human existence is a conflicted existence. The question is what to do so that the human experience becomes more and more a humanized experience, one of people, of individuals, of subjects, not one of objects. And that cannot be achieved without struggle, without hope, without tenacity, and without strength.

How can we face the teaching profession in light of today's rampant lack of hope?
The only path is finding reasons for hope within hopelessness. Hope must be rebuilt. And in order to do that, one must recognize the different times of history, recognize that today the struggle is harder. And if the struggle is much too difficult today, we must even learn to "hibernate." The world will not come to an end in two or three years of waiting. I have no doubt that much of the current hopelessness regarding the shamelessness of this fatalist neoliberal ideology will convert itself into strength of hope as a result of that very shamelessness, that ideological fatalism, which won't last very long.

As regards the hope-hopelessness pair, it is good to be reminded that history does not begin or end with us. I believe it is necessary to be more humble with respect to our individual historical task. Clearly, if I consider myself "the leader," if I believe it is up to me personally to accomplish the mission of changing the world, I may fall into hopelessness. However, if I humbly know that I am one among thousands, that history does not end with my death or with the end of my generation, but that it goes on, I will then understand that even a minimum I may be able to do will have some important result.

What do you understand the educator's ethic to be?
Ethics defines what must be; it establishes the moral principles of sociability and respect; it regulates our presence in the world. In order to avoid the wiles of ideology, I say that ethics has to do with common sense. For example, starting out from that point of view, would it be ethical to exploit people? To discriminate against the different? Would it be right to humiliate or depreciate a student, to subject him or her to irony? To laugh at him or her? To intimidate him or her? From the standpoint of common sense, no one can accept that. Ethicalness is a concrete attitude that does not come from abstract discourse, but rather from living it in all its fairness and plenitude.

In Brazil, there are teachers who encourage their students to be absent from classes when the following day is a holiday. I believe that a teacher who acts in this manner is breaking with ethics. The educative process is above all ethical. It requires from us constant testimony to seriousness.

One of the most beautiful characteristics of a teacher is to testify to his or her students that ignorance is the starting point for knowledge, that making mistakes is no sin, that it is part of the discovery process. Error is an opportunity to seek knowledge. Error is precisely what makes us learn. Do not be embarrassed at not knowing. Many teachers will "shoot in the dark" or "guess," just say any old thing for fear of looking stupid. Do not silence your students so as to keep them from asking questions. Asking questions, doubting, problematizing, dialoguing, is fundamental in the educative act. It suffices to say, "I don't know, but I will try to find out." That is an ethical action on the part of the educator, without which one cannot educate.

When I was a young university professor, a female student asked me a question that I did not know how to answer. I owned up to that naturally: "I don't know, but you can rest assured that if we work together we can find an answer. I invite you, if you are free next Saturday, to have lunch together." She came to my house; we had lunch, spent two or three hours in my private library. We found the answer, and the following class, we informed the others as to our search and our findings. That did not depreciate me; quite the contrary. What the young folks want is proof that they can trust us, and the more serious a teacher is, the more they will believe in him or her.

Notes

1. Gathering held on August 17, 1996, at the San Luís Sports Stadium with 3,500 educators who came from neighboring cities in addition to the educators of San Luís.

2. Mauricio Amílcar López was the first president of the National University of San Luís. Three years after his being appointed, he was expelled from the university by the Argentine military regime. One early morning in 1977, nine armed and hooded men went into his house, in Mendoza, Argentina, and kidnapped him. López is one of the 30,000 political disappearances of the Argentine dictatorship.

Media Interview

The Confrontation Is Not Pedagogical, but Rather Political[1]

IN THE 1960S AND '70S, there was a focus on the great issues of the day, among them the freedom and self-determination of peoples. The subsequent dictatorships choked off this debate at its roots. Should we now return to these issues?
These are the paradoxes of history. On the one hand, it conveys the impression that all these things have been forgotten, that they have been surpassed, and on the other hand, history invites us to ponder these questions once again.

Not long ago, in Brazil, we drew up a list of the problems that my generation had had to face and there were young people of twenty-two, twenty-three years of age who calculated that some of these problems were the same ones they were having to face up to today. The issue here is that problems aren't plucked out of the air, but occur within history, they change with history, so that the solutions we find for these problems are not the same. In other words, as historical time changes, even if the overall problem may still be the same, our methods for tackling it are not necessarily the same.

One of the issues that remains unresolved is the respect for human integrity. As generations change, their sensitivity in this matter may change, but what doesn't change is the need to find new ways to carry on the struggle. So when it seemed

33

that the question of the integrity of the human being was no longer an issue, the problem returned …, and I have no doubt that in ten or fifteen years, the concern for human beings will take on renewed vigor. I'll no longer be here and you, and others like you, will raise similar questions with another Paulo Freire, and will say, "old Freire was right: the struggle to help men and women discover their own *being*, their full potential, will remain with us.…"

In the underdeveloped countries, education is in a state of crisis. How should we face up to this crisis?
Firstly, I don't think the crisis in education is limited to underdeveloped countries. Secondly, I don't think it's a crisis in education alone, but rather one of the whole of society; it's a crisis at the heart of our current socio-economic system, and is inevitably reflected in education. For my part, I have absolutely no doubt whatsoever that the confrontation is not a pedagogical one, but that it is political. I'm not going to change pedagogy by mounting a pedagogical struggle. It's not the philosophers of education who are going to change pedagogy, but the politicians who will do it in response to our pressure, always assuming that we exert pressure on them. Education is an eminently political activity. That's why it's impossible to put into practice a pedagogy that is neutral. At heart, there's no such thing as neutrality. For me, I repeat, this is a political struggle.

And one of the problems we have to face today is how to communicate with the great majority of people who nowadays find themselves divided up into minorities, and therefore have no awareness of themselves as majorities. We have to reinvent ways to communicate, to inter-communicate. I agree with [German sociologist and philosopher Jürgen] Habermas in that I have no doubt that communication is a fundamental issue as this century draws to a close. And it is impossible to think about the theme of communication without, for example, having to consider our intellectual awareness of the world. It is precisely the possibility of understanding the world that allows us to communicate it. For us as educators, the question is how to improve communicability, how to transform it into communication. This is an eminently political task. I'm an optimist. Let me repeat what, for me, is a given: it is difficult to change, but it is possible.

What is your understanding of the situation of the popular sectors of Latin American society in the context of the current politics of neoliberalism?
This is a question that any educator should ask himself. One of the greatest challenges of the moment is how to confront the paralyzing and fatalistic ideology that neoliberal discourse has imposed on us. Two things concerning this subject: the first is that, contrary to what is commonly believed, the great strength of neoliberal discourse resides in its political-ideological rather than in its economic dimension.

In Brazil, this fatalism has spread on a massive scale through both the labor and academic sectors. When I argue that it is unacceptable for us to accept that thirty million Brazilian men and women are dying of hunger, the answer I usually get is, "Paulo, it's tragic, but it's reality." This type of statement is immoral and absurd. This is not reality, but what has become reality. And it has become this not because it wants to. No reality is its own boss. Reality has become like this because, as such, it serves certain interests in the hierarchy of power.

Our struggle must be to change this reality and not accommodate ourselves to it. This postmodern fatalism that didn't exist before is, at heart, the implied intent of neoliberal discourse, and it must be resisted with maximum force. We must remain alert, totally focused; we must get up on Tuesday and ask ourselves whether we didn't surrender to fatalism on Monday.

The other point to emphasize is that this fatalism has created a kind of neoliberal pragmatism in educational practice which, in both popular education and in the regular educational system, can be summed up in a simple sentence that some of you have no doubt heard expressed, for example, as follows: "Paulo Freire's *finished.*" And why is Paulo Freire *finished*? Precisely because of the utopian dimension of his thought. Paulo Freire is *finished* because he maintains a hopeful, utopian position that no longer exists elsewhere.

And what does this neoliberal pragmatism consist of? Of no longer talking about an educator's overall formation, but rather about his or her technical and scientific training. For example, the Faculty of Medicine must focus on the training of surgeons and clinicians, each in their particular specialty. And popular education, in accordance with this same precept, should focus on the productive capacity of craftsmen rather than on their overall formation. This type of discourse makes use of the word "citizenship," but limits it essentially to the notion of productive capacity. On the other hand, as far as we are concerned, a good citizen is a good man or a good woman, and only if they are good men and good women can they also be good doctors or good craftsmen. We are *people* before we are specialists.

My pedagogy continues to be the pedagogy of "peoplification," or "peoplitude." It is focused on forming good people and not just specialists. This is the position we must assume in order to hinder and defeat the advance of the ideology of neoliberalism.

At the heart of this model, which doesn't only seek to exclude the popular classes but most of the middle class as well, do you not think that in the future, the class struggle will involve the appropriation of knowledge?
In the first place, the discourses of so-called post-modernity speak of the death of ideologies, but in fact there is only one way to kill ideology, and that is ideologically. These discourses maintain, for example, that there are no social classes. Very well, I say, to follow up on this same example, let us suppose that there are no more social classes. Well, okay, now let me ask you: is there also no more exploitation? If your answer is that there is no more exploitation, I shall ask you to show me any place in the world where this is true. You won't find one!

Sadly, exploitation is alive and well, and wherever there is exploitation, then there are social classes, too—one the class that exploits, the other the class that is exploited. Exploitation is almost as old as human history.

Still on the subject of social classes, it doesn't matter whether these have another name, for social classes are a product of history, and as such they change with the course of history. It's easier to see the existence of social classes in São Paulo than it is in Geneva, but I can't then conclude that there are no social classes in Geneva. All that's needed is a bit of thoughtful analysis, and we'll be able to identify the social classes of Geneva in five minutes.

Obviously, classes change historically, but they go on existing. This is what I believe. But at the same time, I have absolutely no doubt that sooner than many people ever imagined, the men and women of the world will invent new ways of carrying on the struggle that we cannot, for the moment, envisage. Recently, there was a meeting of European scientists in Berlin, brought together to discuss alternative ways forward in the wake of the situation in Chiapas. It was a meeting that was full of life, of hope, and of resistance, the opposite of neoliberalism. It was there that I suggested that we were now beginning to understand how new forms of rebellion might be devised. I have no doubt that this is going to happen, but I also think I am going to die, much to my sorrow, before being able to witness them. But I have no doubt whatsoever that this process of re-humanization, of "peoplification," will come about.

In the context of this neoliberal fatalism, what are your thoughts with regard to popular education?
In my opinion, there is a whole range of political and pedagogical questions that we should be tackling within the general strategy of what we call "popular education."

This question of stasis and fatalism is obviously one of them. In the late 1950s, I coined a term with which many were unfamiliar: *conscientization*. I have explained on various occasions that I am not the creator of this concept, but I consider myself responsible for our political, pedagogical, and epistemological understanding of the term. One of my most fundamental concerns at that time was to consider conscientization as a particularly radical posture from which to gain an understanding of the world, if we compare it with the posture that we more commonly define as an awareness. In other words, conscientization involves assuming an awareness, but then it deepens it.

When I embarked on my efforts, I was thinking precisely about this question of fatalism. I wanted to combat the paralyzed and paralyzing effects of fatalism among peasants who, in the face of exploitation, tend to explain their situation by ignoring history, explaining it as God's will, a consequence of their sins or their destiny. I kept asking myself how I could make this social group understand that, in the final analysis, culture is the creation of man and woman, of their actions, of their imagining of a world that we did not invent, but that we encountered ready and waiting. I remember that in order to tackle this question, it seemed to me important to deepen, from a critical perspective, the concept of culture. And to say, "If we have been capable of changing the natural world, which we had no part in making, that was already made, if, through our own intervention, we have been able to add something that didn't exist before, why aren't we able to change the world that we *did* make, the world of culture, of politics, of exploitation, and of social class?"

Seen from this perspective, the concept of culture had a profound impact. I cited some of the reactions witnessed in my books. For example, in Brazil, in the half-light of a cultural center, a humble street sweeper listened dumbstruck to what, for him, were unimaginable approaches to the theme of culture, then took to the floor and proclaimed, "From tomorrow, I shall turn up for work with my head held high, my dignity regained, because reality can be changed." I shall never forget his reaction. "Now, I've got hope," he said. With these words, he was telling me two things: on one hand, I have made an effort and understood, and on the other, I'm going to turn up with my head high and my dignity regained, because reality can be changed. Another incredible instance was that of a woman who held up a clay vase she had made, and proudly proclaimed, "This is my culture."

Faced with conscientization, fatalism collapses. That is why, nowadays, when the "pragmatists" of neoliberalism say, "Paulo Freire is *finished*," I don't take offense, and tell them with absolute conviction, "No! Paulo Freire isn't *finished*. Paulo Freire is still here." And he's still here because history is here, waiting for us to do something with it, waiting for us to confront the fatalistic culture of neoliberalism, which maintains, for example, that the number of unemployed in the world is a fatalistic consequence of this century's end. This is what university professors, sociologists, and political scientists tell us. How is it possible for people in universities to tell us that unemployment is a product of fate? What have they been reading? What is the basis of their logic? No! Nothing is fatalistically determined in the world of culture.

When people ask me about popular education, my proposals are, for the most part, not far removed from what I was propounding in the 1960s, by which I mean, working with the most deprived groups in *favelas*,² in rural settlements, helping people to understand that there is no such thing as fatalism in human behavior, that history is what we ourselves make, and what in turn makes us. But for history to make us, it was necessary for us to make it first. History can't come before men and women because history is a cultural product. It was by creating history that men and women made themselves in history.

So what we need to do is to discuss again the concept of the conscientization of subjects as makers of history. There is no more crucial moment than this in the formation of an autonomous subject. And there is no more effective moment in neoliberal discourse than that in which subjects accept themselves as mere objects because they consider this to be inevitable. We must carry on the struggle. We must combat through all possible means this fatalism as a first step toward some later adjustment.

Notes

1. Interview with the press of San Luís, Argentina, August 18, 1996.
2. Ghettos or slums.

PART II

CHILE

Interviews with Boris Bezama[1]

Unafraid to Love

Boris Bezama: He is a subversive, even though he describes himself as postmodern, but of the sort who believes in utopias. He is a critic of the sectarian, dogmatic left of the 1970s. An educationalist and a militant of the Workers' Party in Brazil, Freire is "the primary teacher of the poor."

His methods for disseminating literacy helped thousands of people discover and conquer the magical world of putting letters together. His books have been translated into over twenty languages and are obligatory reading in the realm of popular education.

After an absence of twenty years, he has returned to Chile, more youthful than ever. His vitality belies his wrinkles and his white hair, and although he is now seventy, he is capable of restoring anyone's hope. It's what happened on the day he gave a lecture at the El Canelo de Nos Center, during the opening of the Festival of Creativity.

"I am passion, feelings, fears, doubts, desires, I am utopias, I am projects" is how Paulo Freire defines himself.

He lived in Chile after the 1964 coup in Brazil. "The doctrine of national security will spread through the whole continent, and Chile won't be an exception," he affirmed before the Chilean coup. He currently teaches in a postgraduate program at the Catholic University of São Paulo, and is finishing the new prologue to Pedagogy of the Oppressed,[2] *as well as another two books. He was an advisor to the World Council of Churches and, until a few months ago, held a post of considerable responsibility in the São Paulo municipal administration.*

Bezama: From school right through to parliament, there is a lack of coherence between what is said and what is done. Might this be one of the reasons for the loss of faith in the governing classes in Latin America?

Paulo Freire: There is indeed a huge gap between what is said and what is done. But I would rather see a thousand politicians saying one thing and doing another than a coup d'état being prepared in secret. It's better to have a Congress full of contradictions than a Congress that has been silenced by the military intent on "saving us" yet again. A month ago, in Brazil, I watched a discussion on television, in which a senator from the government party accused the opposition of trying to ensure the government failed. A member of the parliamentary opposition denied the charge and replied that they were moved solely by their duty to make sure that the campaign pledges made by President Fernando Collor de Melo were kept, even though he knew that he would, in fact, be unable to keep them. The senator's immediate retort was that campaign rhetoric consisted in "saying what wouldn't be done in order to win."

This statement isn't the norm, but rather anecdotal. However, it's better to experience this type of *counter-pedagogy* than that other type of situation that all Latin America has had to face. In any event, it's precisely these unethical instances that enable progressive people like ourselves to forge ahead in order to change society. When humans cease to dream, they die. Pragmatists accuse us of being romantics because we seek to transform the world and refuse to adapt to this unjust reality.

Bezama: Are you that type of romantic who still believes in the guerrilla struggle and seizing power?

Freire: No. I don't believe the madness of the 1970s can be repeated. But it's one thing to criticize these methods and another to switch sides and accommodate yourself to immobility.

Bezama: This doesn't seem to be the best time for the left.
Freire: This is the best time for progressives because we face a new challenge: to understand that the form of socialism that was actualized was a sinister, necrophiliac experience, that loved death rather than life, that was dictatorial, sectarian, incapable of coexisting with that which was different. But nothing in this world should be considered the definitive model. That socialism failed yesterday doesn't mean that it will fail again tomorrow. As progressives, our task is to assume responsibility for our past mistakes, but by assuming them, we do not need to abandon our progressive ideas, unless, of course, we abdicate them completely. History is not homogeneous, and we should create the future by transforming the present with the experience of the past. History hasn't ended. No one can decree its end. If this were to occur, then a term would have to be invented to evoke such a fact. Dreams are not only the stuff of political life, but are also part of human existence. Reactionaries also dream and fight to preserve that which cannot be preserved. I continue to dream, full of faith and hope in social transformation. What should be done is to redefine people's capacity for reading history.

Bezama: But the left used to insist on an exhaustive reading of reality. Who can be sure that it won't make the same mistake again?
Freire: I don't think it did very much at all. Left-wing organizations thought history was on their side. "History is with us," they would say, as if history were a servant of the left. Many people believed in a kind of easy-to-control dialectic through which we would arrive at socialism. This was merely a falsification of that which we were really seeking. We were in thrall to its arrogance and authoritarianism. But now, after the lessons

learned from our own experiences as well as from the countries of the Eastern Bloc, we must accept diversity.

*Bezama: Having witnessed so many changes in the world, how do
you feel now that you have reached the age of seventy?*
Freire: Very youthful, because I am always open to learning,
to gaining new wisdom and new knowledge. I experience
these three things every day. A person stays like this when
he or she is not afraid to love, and when he or she doesn't
fear starting all over again. I can't understand my life without
love. I am in love again. I'm in love with her, Nita, because
of her angelic way. I detest the puritanism of those who are
smitten with horror when they see a woman with a beautiful
pair of legs, seductively crossed. They are horrified because
they would like to sin. Puritanism is the frightful corruption
of purity. For me, a puritan is an old person, even if they is
eighteen years old. And women or men who cut themselves
off, are indifferent to the world around them, who don't
question things. Questioning oneself is a quality inherent
in humankind. Those who don't question are dead. People
retain their youth when they throw themselves into the process of seeking and creating.

Educating for Freedom

Bezama: Twenty years after writing Pedagogy of the Oppressed,
*what are the changes that have occurred with regard to the issues you
raised in your book, and how would you define education on the eve
of a new millennium?*
Freire: I still think that education needs to provide a process of
transformation that allows men and women to become liber-
ated. It continues to suffer from the perversity of the system,
from the incompetence of its methodology and a huge ideological burden that causes students to be seen as a "problem."
In Brazil, eight million children are outside the system and
there is a reason why this is so.

I put forward the proposition in *Pedagogy of the Oppressed* that education can never be neutral, but is political. Apart from this, there is no educational practice without ethics or aesthetics. We need to respect the student's cultural identity and we must teach him or her to learn. A system of education based on the weighty accumulation of facts learnt by heart and of no relevance to the student's future life is of no use at all.

Bezama: How is it possible to put into effect a progressive education in our countries, where authoritarianism is built into our educational system?
Freire: To answer this question, we need to accept that history is neither linear nor homogeneous. If it were always the same, it would be very boring. There would be no room for emotion or uncertainty.

Progressive education has its dreams, its objectives, its targets to be striven for, its methods and its limitations. Now, putting into effect progressive education varies historically from context to context. It is one thing to teach in the Brazil of the present, as it was another to try to institute progressive education during the dictatorship. It is one thing to teach in the northeast of Brazil, and another to work in Chile or in Switzerland. In other words, each case is different, it is historical, and it changes from one age to another, one location to another. In these circumstances, educators who are favorable to change should understand the way historical facts occur, and never forget their utopian dreams. And so in spite of the current considerable limitations in the Latin American educational system, there is a crucial need for renovation, not only for our children, but also for society as a whole, which anxiously awaits these changes.

We cannot proceed pragmatically in educational practice, in the act of educating, from a utilitarian standpoint. On the contrary, we must educate by assuming a progressive position, discovering the existing limitations, the obstacles that lie before us, and in this way we must take up the challenges that will enable us to achieve freedom.

Now, if society is going through a social and historical experience that is far removed from a climate of greater freedom, progressive education should devise methods that are appropriate to these limitations.

Bezama: Yet, current education is becoming more and more remote from the values of a humanist society. This is what suits the neoliberal system.

Freire: But this doesn't mean that history has ended. Neoliberalism has its historical epoch. And apart from this, I'm not obliged to be a neoliberal just because its doctrine has a certain powerful influence nowadays, just as I never accepted Stalinism when any criticism of that political path meant that one was bourgeois, of which, in my case, I was often accused.

Bezama: Do you consider that the educational crisis that we are currently going through is due to the numerous changes and new technologies that have not been adopted in schools?

Freire: No. My understanding is that the crisis we are experiencing in education is a political crisis, a crisis in the structure of the State and of society. On the other hand, there is no doubt that transformations that have occurred outside school ought to be incorporated into the school system. But—and this is my warning—it's a mistake to assume that computers alone can educate.

What I do think is important is that we study ways and means to introduce an inter-disciplinary curriculum into the school system, for we need to have a more or less global vision of reality, instead of a vision that is compartmentalized and fragmentary.

Notes

1. Boris Bezama is an important and respected Chilean journalist, currently contributing to the Santiago daily *Diario de la nación.* These

two interviews were published in the semimonthly magazine *Educación* (December 23, 1991–January 5, 1992, pp. 22–23, Santiago, Chile). Paulo gave these interviews during a visit to the country that gave him refuge for four years when he needed to go into exile during the Brazilian coup of 1964. This was the only journey he made to Chile during the regime of the dictator Augusto Pinochet.

　　2. The prologue grew so long and complex that Paulo decided to turn it into a new book, which was published with the title of *Pedagogy of Hope: A Re-Encounter with Pedagogy of the Oppressed* (São Paulo: Paz e Terra, 1992).

PART III

NICARAGUA

Manifesto

Ten Years of the People's Sandinista Revolution[1]

As an educator, who has been dedicating his life to the construction of a Pedagogy of the Oppressed, to write about the ten years of the People's Sandinista Revolution is cause for considerable emotion. That is because in our Nicaragua— I put it this way to express how much we feel part of this revolution—many fellow Latin American educators' dreams are being realized, educators who are striving to achieve an educational practice profoundly rooted in the struggle of the people, that may make itself felt in all spheres of social life and contribute to that which is most irreversible in a revolution, namely, the *Insurrection of Consciousness*, to use the title of that magnificent work by Orlando Nuñez.

The educational priority of this revolution made itself felt immediately in the wake of the triumph of July 19, 1979, when the political decision was made to embark on that wonderful National Literacy Crusade, which, apart from achieving an impressive reduction in the rate of illiteracy, became a vast movement in mobilization and education, not only among those entering literacy but also among the literate, who together developed their awareness of Nicaraguan reality, and as a consequence, an awareness of how they might transform it. There then followed efforts to construct an educational system in the country that might incorporate the wealth of experiences developed within the people's organizations and during the Literacy Crusade itself.

The educational character of the practical progress of this revolution was also felt in the out-and-out concern with recuperating the historical and cultural memory of popular struggle. This has contributed to the constitution of a national identity that enables you to affirm, for example, that it is not possible to be a Marxist in Nicaragua without being at the same time a Sandinista, and that has enabled the incorporation of Christians in the revolutionary struggle to serve as an example and a vehicle for questioning many of those who have become embedded in a dogmatic and doctrinaire interpretation of Marxism.

It is in the deep-felt conviction of this revolution, and above all in its democratic practice, that we can find enlightened teaching for popular struggle. The popular content and revolutionary practice of democracy, understood as a strategic value, renders possible educational practices and, above all, provides an indispensable opportunity and flexibility for a revolutionary process that is forged in the responses to concrete reality and to the needs and aspirations of the people.

It is in this context that what seems to be the greatest strength of this revolution is shaped: the moral and ethical strength of its people, capable of heroically confronting the criminal interference of North American imperialism and the severe economic and social consequences that this provokes.

In the words of the anthem of the FSLN [Sandinista Front for National Liberation], this people "does not yield and does not sell itself," but marches on with great courage, joy, and democracy, creating its popular revolution, which enlightens us and reinvigorates us in our educational practices and the people's commitment to the struggle for freedom of all the peoples of Latin America.

—São Paulo, August 8, 1989

Note

1. The Nicaraguan people had to suffer the dictatorship of the Somoza family from the 1930s onward. In the '70s, guerrilla groups of various political tendencies—communists, social democrats, and liberals—formed the *Frente Sandinista* (Sandinista Front), and fought against Somoza's dictatorship. The "People's Sandinista Revolution" triumphed on July 19, 1979. However, the *Frente Sandinista* survived for only a few years with its initial objectives intact. In the '80s, at the height of the revolution, Paulo visited the country and contributed to the reconstruction of Nicaragua with his critical understanding of education, especially in the National Literacy Crusade.

PART IV

PARAGUAY

Discussion Seminar with Paulo Freire[1]

Popular Education in Latin America: Contextualization and Possibilities within Transition Processes

I would like to begin this morning by once again emphasizing my open position with regard to differences. This does not mean that I defend a position that is excessively empty, bland, and accommodating, with which anyone can agree with everything in order to appear always polite and courteous. This is not my position. I defend the struggle, I struggle hard on behalf of my dreams and in defense of my ideas. But I have a profound respect for positions that are opposed to my own.

When you ask me to talk a little about popular education in Latin America at the present time, I would like to make it clear that what I will say does not necessarily accord with your position or that of others, but it is one that may be democratically debated. It is my position, but that doesn't mean that it is the most correct, or that it is the only one: other truths exist as well.

In talking about popular education, I would begin by formulating a question relating to the expression "popular education." We have two words here: one that functions at the level of our thought process, within the structure of our thought, or that performs the task of a noun, *education*. This noun relates to a particular activity, to a particular practice that suggests we understand popular education as a whole, that we understand this noun, *education*, within the general context of *popular education.*

Secondly, we see that this general contextual term possesses another word, an adjective: *popular*, alongside which my noun, *education*, is defined as having a particular quality. And there's one more thing: it is precisely because of this particular quality that I felt obliged to use the adjective *popular*. This particular quality that the adjective adds to the concept enshrined in the noun *education* does not necessarily form part of the general character attributed to that noun. If it did, there would be no reason to say *popular*.

And so, faced with this initial thought, faced with this initial analysis, I realize that it is not just about any education, but a particular education that I termed *popular*, and that means it would also be possible to have other adjectives to qualify the noun *education*. I could, for example, utter or write down my thoughts on *elitist education*, and in this case, *elitist* would function in exactly the same way. That is to say that I would be giving or adding a particular quality to the substantive character of the word *education* in order to mark or demarcate the field of activity about which I had spoken. In the same way, I could say reflections on *authoritarian education*, or on *democratic education*, for example.

Well, this now invites or even obliges me to ponder a while on education itself, without its qualifying adjective, before explaining what I mean by popular education. In other words, I shall pause briefly to reflect on the substantiveness that the noun suggests: What is this practice that I call education? What are the most visible elements that contribute to this practice?

Elements in Education

As a primal experience, a first shot at an answer might lead me to conclude that education is a vital experience, an experience that occurs in a world that is alive, but not in any live world.

This seems obvious to me, given that it isn't even necessary to check whether a practice can exist in a nonvital world; at the very least it has so far been impossible to identify something we might recognize as education within such a world. There are different levels of life, and I note that it is only in the sphere of human life that education has become established. I can't, for example, in all seriousness, talk about education among trees. As much as I love trees, it would be extremely difficult to prove that trees are educated, although they are, of course, cultivated.

They are cultivated by us, and also by themselves.... Trees communicate with one another; they also possess a certain type of language, as recent research has demonstrated. Among other animals, but not ourselves, what happens is a process of habilitation rather than a pedagogical practice. For this reason, it would be very difficult to organize a meeting of dogs, for example: for the dogs in the area to meet and play host to Paulo Freire, while debating the most effective ways to defend the master of the house. No, this has never happened. On the other hand, dogs communicate with one another.

Education is presented, among men and women, on one hand as a necessity, and on the other as a quality that we gain historically throughout the whole course of our social experience. Historically, not in the sense of merely preserving life, education also has a very clear initial purpose, which is to transmit from one generation to another its cultural elements, its forms of defense. Education has therefore always been, and still is, one of our inventions.

So the education that occurs among us occurs only among us, human beings.

Education implies certain objectives, certain concrete aims that I tend to call our dreams, and that presuppose the existence of active agents or subjects. It implies a certain content, a certain object that, from the teacher's point of view, needs to be taught, and from that of the pupil, needs to be learned. These dreams therefore go beyond education itself, beyond the actual educational practice. So, these are dreams of subjects that exercise educational practice between subjects and recognizable objects that go to constitute the content of education. These objects that, on one hand, influence the subjects should be taught by the men and women who teach, and on the other, should be learned by the men and women who are being educated.

I propose that we think about something very basic, to give serious understanding to what it means to teach, what it means to learn. In order for us to be able to understand what it is to teach and to learn, we must first be able to gain an understanding of the stages of a much bigger process: the process of gaining knowledge.

The educator needs to use certain procedures through which to approach, for better or worse, and with more or less rigor, the object that he is teaching, and in so teaching, he relearns and reacquaints himself with what he already knew. In this way, his task of teaching is a task that, while he teaches, he remembers, relearns, reunderstands, and thus enables his pupils to gain understanding. While the pupils therefore seek to understand, the educators are reunderstanding the object they are teaching.

It is impossible for educational practice to exist without these elements being linked. It has never existed, any more than it can ever exist in the future. When we try to make ourselves aware of this, we realize and understand that when an educator doesn't know why she or he is an educator, doesn't understand the struggle she or he is involved in, there is a tendency to become bureaucratic. Quite simply, it is a question of earning a good or bad salary while seeking something better. But it happens that if I am an educator, I should be clear about the utopia that is precisely the reason for my dream, a dream that relates to society itself, to the social and political life of which I am a part.

In other words, as I said yesterday, What is the profile of an educator? What is the project for social, economic, and political life that I hold dear, as do many men and women educators, not in order to mold young people and adults, but to stand alongside them in defense of our dream?

It is precisely because there is no education without this, without a dream, that we are told education is always directive. Many people have criticized me, saying that I was not directive, which is a mistaken interpretation of me as a person, and of the work that I have been doing for decades. One must not confuse the directorial character of education with manipulation. I am directorial, but not manipulative. Directivity explains exactly why there can never be neutrality in education. Education never has been neutral and it certainly can't be now. But its non-neutrality doesn't mean that I should be authoritarian just because I am directorial. Directivity can and should be democratic, or better said, I follow the path of directivity democratically, because there are those educators, both women and men, who tread the same path in a manipulative way. That is why we can and should say, This is democratic education and that is authoritarian education. Authoritarian education is that whose directivity is taken possession of by the educator (who therefore holds the reins) and, in this way, manipulates the pupils by exercising his power; democratic education, on the other hand, is that in which there is no manipulation, unless as a contradiction.

This is, therefore, a dimension we encounter when we ask ourselves about education as a quality, as a practice; it is the experience of educators and educatees being together, mediated by the object they seek to acquaint or reacquaint themselves with, and to go beyond purely the experience of teaching and learning that, in the final analysis, constitutes the directivity of education.

I believe that one of the main duties of educators working with their pupils and students is to witness their respect, their respect for themselves. For example, in all honesty, I can tell you that I know many people who do this, but I see a contradiction, for example, in a democratic, conscientious teacher who is certain in her dreams, but who, in her behavior toward her students, doesn't convey a sense of serious intent and respect. Primarily, respect for herself, but also for her students. She may, for example, arrive in class looking disheveled. Of course, a classroom isn't a beauty parlor, nor should it involve a fashion parade, but I do believe that educators, whether men or women, should look after their appearance as best as they can. They should always be clean, have a pretty dress, tidy clothing; they should dress modestly, but decently. And what I mean by decency doesn't have anything to do with puritanism, but with aesthetics.

Aesthetics are closely associated with ethics, beauty, and decency; there's no getting away from this if one wants to be a good educator. That is why I said a classroom isn't a place for a fashion show, all the more so given the very poor salaries, which means that a teacher can't dress herself in the latest fashion from Paris. But with cheap clothing it is possible to be well dressed. I believe that this manifestation of a like for beauty, of an acceptance of beauty, is absolutely crucial.

In sum, the classroom, the school, is a space and a time in which to display respect for self and for others. A place for serious activity, without being closed. One needs to celebrate the joy of living while also being serious. One needs to be rigorous while remaining an open *being*. One must be a sincere, ethical *human being*.

Education is an act in which a process of gaining knowledge is developed. There is no education without knowledge, and knowledge occurs through the educator's act of teaching and the educatee's act of learning. But the educatee learns only when he learns the object and not when he receives the description of the object and commits it to memory by rote.

Education is political and may be democratic, just as it may be elitist and authoritarian. This is why it is not neutral, but depends on the option taken. On one hand, the educator's political option depends on the coherence that the educator has with respect to his or her option. But we need to face the fact that authoritarian practice is very common, above all when we pass through a phase of political transition that is full of incoherencies, because after forty years of dictatorship, it's not easy for us to attain some sort of equilibrium that may overcome our fear of speaking, our fear of criticizing. It's not easy to overcome a predisposition to give orders—when someone has the slightest degree of power, he feels himself equal to a general. In our countries, the doorman at a party can display the same arbitrary behavior as a general when he leads a coup d'état. It is really quite incredible. It doesn't matter what the rank is—general, colonel, corporal, sergeant, or private—all of them, given a modicum of authority, exert the tightest of grips upon it.

All education is political; this is unavoidable. But this doesn't mean that educators should impose their party's agenda on those they are educating. One thing is the politicization of education and another is the educator's choice of party. I have no right whatsoever to impose my preference for the party I support in Brazil upon the men and women I am educating. But I have a duty to tell them what that party is. This business of insisting that the educator must keep his distance so as not to influence his educatees is, as far as I am concerned, profoundly flawed. I have no doubt at all that the great respect I have for my educatees is shown in the way I convey to them the energy with which I struggle to uphold my ideals. This is educational. But at the same time, I must show deep respect for the ideals for which they strive as men and women, even if they are very different from my own, because if I am adamant and forbid them to express themselves, then I am being authoritarian, incoherent, and my pedagogical theories are hypocritical.

And so, in an age of political transition, one of the greatest challenges we must face is to see how we may move forward, and this moving forward is not achieved by speeches alone. We have to develop a practice that is contrary to the authoritarian tradition, and to reflect critically on this practice in order to understand precisely where we are going wrong.

All this you already knew, but I'm repeating it here as a question of method, in order to emphasize this: that it is not possible to understand education if one ignores these elements.

What Is Popular Education?

Now that I am convinced that education is a task for us humans, that education is not neutral, I understand very clearly why it is termed *popular education*.

I ask myself this: what is it that I seek to express, exactly, when I say *popular education*?

The adjective *popular* refers to the people and not the elite. *People*, in the broadest sense, has nothing to do with the ruling classes. When we say *people*, we are not including the industrialists within this concept, by which I do not mean to say that the industrialists are not included in another understanding of the concept of "people," namely, the people of a country. I don't have the power to separate them as they do with regard to us. But from a sociological and political point of view, they are obviously not "the people."

When I say *popular education*, I am referring to education for a certain type of social class.

Popular education refers first and foremost to the education of the popular classes. It is therefore related to an education that we could term, using a more religious language, "education of the poor." I don't like this expression, but it refers precisely to the education of the oppressed, the education of the deceived, the education of the forbidden. At least, that's how I think of it.

Precisely because that is how I think of it, when I talk of popular education, I try to put across the idea that this popular education is, first and foremost, at the service of the popular classes, or of their interests, without this implying the denial of the rights of the elites. I'm not saying that we should kill rich children, or deny them an education. No, not at all. But the major objective of popular education lies precisely in attending to the interests of the popular classes, who have been denied these rights over the last 500 years.

Secondly, precisely because I have discovered, within the concept of popular education, this practical aim in defending their interests, working to defend these interests, I also discover that I would like popular education, in its practice, to contribute in some way to the radical transformation of society in order that the popular classes may gain political presence, political influence, leadership, within the new power base that we need to create.

From a more radical point of view, popular education, for me, means ways forward—that is, ways forward into the field of knowledge and into the field of politics, through which—and this is where utopia comes into it—the popular classes might achieve power. This is what popular education means, for me; what it meant in the '60s, what it meant in the '70s, what it meant in the '80s, and what it means now, as well. And neoliberal discourse has no room for this. It has nothing to do with it at all. For me, one of the greatest risks that we are running today, we progressive men and women, lies in the fact that we are feeling exhausted, existentially exhausted, because of so much lack of success, so many coups, the fall of Eastern Europe, the famous death of Marx, the widely proclaimed death of socialism. One of the risks some or many of us run is to surrender ourselves to the lullaby of neoliberalism and fall asleep in the arms of the neoliberals, who tell us that we should no longer think about living, that popular education nowadays should equip the poor for finding work. This is what is explicit in neoliberal discourse.

Now, you might say, "But Paulo, don't you agree with training in professional skills?" I do. It is obvious that in the type of education for the power structure that we are intent on defending, we take the training of workers very seriously. For instance, if we are working with a group of builders, it is important that we train a builder to be the best in his trade; but this priority in professional formation does not replace the objective of popular education, because there is another priority that closely accompanies it, without which our concept of liberation cannot work. It is limited to working within the concept of domestication.

The other priority is precisely that which deals with the general history of builders, the general history of the working class, the relations between men and women, technology, politics, the right to intervene, to reforge civil society. This is also the fundamental objective, the fundamental priority of the practice of popular education nowadays in Latin America and anywhere else in the world.

The Challenge of Critical Reflection

I have noticed, I don't know whether you have too, that in some parts of Latin America people say that Freire's days are over, and this is also part of neoliberal discourse. It has been said that what we've got to do now is to focus popular education on productive activities, through cooperatives or some other such thing. I've just got this to say: Do this, but please don't limit popular education to this. If twenty people eat better, it would be madness to feel sad because of it, but we shouldn't rest on our laurels. A proponent of popular education who is a genuine progressive should, for example, continue the debate about the risks of being shoehorned into the capitalist system. For there is no doubt that a group, a cooperative in production and consumption within the capitalist system, will be capitalist, and as such will harm its members. Of that you can be sure ... absolutely sure. It will act in the same way toward its members, and according to the same logic used by the boss toward his employees, because this all forms part of the natural logic of capitalism, which is blind to any alternative to itself. Look, God causes miracles, but not absurd ones; he will not transform capitalism into a more humane way of going about things. No, not even God can do this, because God has a logic that He himself respects. Some bishops and popes may have tried, but certainly not God.

This is why I think as I do, and I apologize for my apparent lack of humility, but I still maintain that Freire's days aren't over, just as the days of anyone who defends a dialectical position aren't over, a progressive position, a position that isn't taken in by these "siren songs" we have to listen to nowadays … by these speeches. And so, now just as before, the challenge to reflect critically upon history, the challenge to gain a more critical awareness of how society works and functions, these are the central concerns of popular education. In Latin America—or anywhere else—we could find umpteen elements that contribute to this critical engagement of the popular classes in search of power and of the reinvention of power. It's not enough merely to take power; power needs to be re-created.

I believe that you are nurturing one of the virtues of this struggle, according to some of the reports I have read. For example, the tolerance, which you told me about yesterday. In societies such as ours that have experienced uninterrupted periods of authoritarianism, intolerance is a terrible thing. The intolerant person always rejects that which is different; it's enough to be different for the intolerant individual to not accept you.

This is absolutely absurd, firstly because people have a right to be different. Secondly, because the world would be completely unbearable if everyone were the same. I would certainly not enjoy being alive if everybody were like me. I've got to be myself, just as I am, and different from the rest.

But returning to the subject of Freire's days being over, I insist that the opposite is true, because the days when we need to be critically aware of the world are far from over. But we should not confuse critical awareness with rationalism. It's not a question of reducing human experience to Cartesian rationalism. Not at all. On the other hand, it's not a question of seeking total knowledge of the world. Nowadays, we have discovered that this is impossible, but we cannot deny that an exercise in transformation requires a political affirmation that, in turn, requires a choice, or by requiring a political choice, induces a process of rupture. There's no choice without rupture and there's no rupture without a decision; there's no decision without making a choice and there's no making a choice without making a comparison; there's no comparison without assessment and there's no assessment without knowledge of the negative and positive outcomes.

So the process of transformation is aesthetic, ethical, political, and knowledge-building. It implies that I should become ever more knowledgeable, not only of the object I wish to transform, but of the reasons why I should transform it, and the outcome to be achieved by transforming it. This also implies that I need to know something more than the object itself. So all this points to a critical exercise in understanding the world; a clarity of thought rather than pure passion, which must also exist, because it is with my body and soul that I embark on the struggle for change: it involves passion, my desire, my frustration, my fears, etc., etc., but also my knowledge. So in this sense, Freire's days aren't over. If someone can prove to me that it is possible to develop a process of transformation without any concern for knowledge, ethics, aesthetics, then I'll withdraw all my books from the publishers, and I'll address the world as follows: "My days really are over." But no one can prove this. Now, we need to change our work procedures, our sectarian readings of the world, the way we approach issues; all this has to be constantly reinvented and I would say that for these things, there can be no prescribed ways. We need to do all this.

I believe I have at least told you my position. On the other hand, I am completely open to change. I hope, after the publication of the book that I've just finished, that there will be many critical observations made because I criticize in the harshest terms possible this type of neoliberalism, with its sugared, slippery, deceitful discourse that is aimed at us, and I'll tell you this: that my socialist dream is stronger than ever. My utopia comes through from my childhood and is full of life, of inspiration, and of dreams. I've written 250 pages of a book all about this,[2] but if you can convince me that I'm wrong, then I'll change.

Interview

[The interview begins with a number of questions put to and answered by Paulo.]

Session One

First Round of Questions
One of the fundamental aspects for education, and particularly in our case, is its close association with the economy. You touched on this, sir, but I'd like you to develop this theme.

We have numerous problems in educational work and one of these involves the technological aspect. How can we, in the sphere of popular education, but also in the academic educational system, face the problems surrounding technology, when we have so many other problems to resolve?

I think Freire's exposé gives a ray of hope and we can see Paulo Freire's youthfulness in it. Basically, I think we all dream of utopia. I think a critically important theme, especially in our times, is that of the negotiations we are going to make in order to achieve this utopia. When we talk of negotiations, these are the concrete negotiations on what popular education is, based in the political and social climate in which we find ourselves.

I think popular education is weak in one aspect: it doesn't offer us clear models for an alternative society. Even though popular education may awaken the awareness of a wide sector, it doesn't offer us a model for society. So this sector copies existing models and therefore fails. This is why I say popular education is weak in one aspect and we run the risk of organizing groups that have undergone a process of conscientization, copying or being receptive to party political programs (of either the left or other sympathies) as models that took root in other times and places. And so I propose that we reflect on this matter.

I would like Paulo to expand on his concept of tolerance and diversity.

Paulo Freire's Answers

The economic aspect

Obviously, I acknowledge the strength of the economic aspect, and not only in education. Many people are mistaken when they think they can create projects of an aesthetic character, of a pedagogical or social character, without considering the economic bases that determine whether these projects are viable. The economic basis is crucial for discussing this topic for two reasons: Firstly, because it is also crucial for formulating my idea and conditioning my personal individual commitment, and all our personal individual commitments. Secondly, because without money we cannot provide education, we cannot provide anything at all. One of the things we would have to do within an obviously progressive policy formulation would be to alter the orientation of public expenditure, the policy governing public spending, and clearly this cannot be done by the administrator alone. For instance, I remember all the problems Luiza Erundina had when she tried to redirect public spending as mayor of São Paulo. As the executive power she was able to do many things, but one cannot do anything if one does not have the legislative and judicial powers on one's side.

But it is not only necessary to redirect public spending policy, but also the policy governing employment conditions and the expectations placed upon those who have been contracted to work, but who don't always work. According to legislation, upheld by the Brazilian Constitution, a whole host of employees are safe from dismissal. So it is absolutely crucial that the time management of these people should be redefined, given that there are an awful lot of people paid a lot of public money without, in fact, doing any work.

When I began as secretary for education, the first resolution I passed was to summon all those on salaries paid by the Secretariat for Education to report for work within three days. I was pressured on all sides to "turn a blind eye" and leave things as they were, but I refused to do this. I told one person, for example, "You were appointed as a teacher, you have ten years' experience, you can't be dismissed, but you should be at your place of work," to which she replied, "But I live in Brasilia." So I said, "Leave your work in Brasilia and come and work here."

There are, nevertheless, moments when a change in policy direction with regard to public expenditure is not enough, and here we have to face the actual question of production. It is true that the economic development of our countries here in Latin America faces many problems, many obstacles, and this affects everything. But if, apart from this, there is no redirecting in the way money is spent, then there is no way in which we can work. And education is something that implies investment. Education cannot be done without spending money; no matter how little one spends, how creative someone is in making use of recyclable materials, and no matter how many good ideas may emerge, money is needed, and educators need to be well paid.

I believe that rhetoric about teacher training, scientific discourse, as well as the rhetoric that gives esteem to the role of educators, are all empty if the educator doesn't have the means to feed himself adequately, to live in satisfactory accommodations, etc. Material considerations are basic, absolutely basic. For how can a teacher improve her scientific knowledge if she doesn't earn enough to even buy a newspaper? How can she, from time to time, read a book? We need to be aware of these questions.

In 1990, the Secretariat for Culture during Erundina's tenure as mayor, and whose director was one of the great Brazilian philosophers, Marilena Chauí, spent some thousands of dollars to renovate and modernize public libraries, and in order to do this, it was necessary to reallocate public funds. But we should consider a government department as a political-ideological adjunct rather than a purely technical adjunct of financial policy. Read a budget proposal, and through it you will see the ideological profile of a government, of a government that spends 1,000 dollars over four years on books and

200 million on the salaries of highly specialized functionaries who don't do any work.

Moreover, I'm deeply worried by the economic question for the following reasons: on one hand, and basically acknowledging one element in production, I wouldn't say a *determining element* because not even Marx would put it like this, but certainly a conditioning element of the substructure is education; and on the other, because in order to develop an educational system that is less bad, we need to invest money in the skills acquisition of its employees. But in addition to all this we have to consider the question of the intellectual formation of the educator and, before anything else, bring about the birth of a new type of educator. In this sense, not much is being done. It's a question for the next hundred years, and we should have started a long time ago.

The technological aspect
The technological aspect is also interesting and plays a leading part in postmodern discourse in the educational sector. I'm going to discuss two points: The first is ideology. The second is technology as an expression of an ideological choice to reduce all educational practice to technological practice. It is no coincidence that North American universities place great emphasis on the departments of technological education. Mind you, I'm not saying we shouldn't make use of technology. On the contrary, I believe men and women should reflect their times, and nowadays, it's not possible for an educator to deny the uses of a computer, videos, and the countless technological elements that can help him in his teaching. I have, for instance, been invited to an international conference in March of next year in Boston, by one of the founding fathers of the use of technology as a means to a more humane society, Professor Seymour Papert, of MIT, who works on computer programs for children. The meeting will discuss the question of technology and education: what to do and how to work with both things. In the final analysis, I believe, firstly, that education cannot be reduced to technology; secondly, we need to create new channels of

knowledge, new methodologies, new relationships between the subjects who seek knowledge and the most advanced technological innovations that we have at our disposal.

I know that one thing can't be separated from the other, but in my view, the most substantive aspect of the question is the first, namely, the relegation of education to a mere exercise of technology. Education makes use of technology, but it is more than technology. Secondly, I believe that the use of technical aids and materials is indispensable; the educator has to free up his or her imagination in order to invent umpteen things with the children. Sometimes there are no toys, but it is possible to make toys. The problem is that we live so far removed from the concrete possibilities enshrined in popular culture that we don't know how to use the creative elements that these possibilities possess, and that are also technical.

Not long ago, a female educator told me, laughing, that a little boy had been submitted to a battery of tests in order to measure his rhythmic aptitude, and that these tests had indicated that he had difficulties in rhythm and that he didn't have the capacity to learn. For that reason, he couldn't embark on a literacy program. Just imagine: he had no rhythm, so he had motor difficulties, etc., and she told me that when she was reading the result of the test, the kid, who was accompanied by his mother, was whistling and dancing, beating out the rhythm of the samba with a box of matches. The boy was "composing" the room with his body and the tests considered him incapable. So the school's ignorance in relation to what the pupil can do is really tragic, and to me, this shows, firstly, an ideological dimension that suggests that teachers are undergoing a kind of historical-cultural-ideological-political-social psychoanalysis that may allow them to discover deep within themselves traces of the dominant ideology, according to which children from the lower social classes are ontologically incompetent. If the child is from the lower social classes, then he or she is inherently incompetent in all activities and therefore cannot learn to read, etc. Many teachers hold this belief—not the majority, but a significant proportion. It was one of the major arguments I had when I was secretary of education in the city of São Paulo: to encourage teachers to admit to or to reveal the elitist ideology that had been injected into each one of them. I think that while teachers are undergoing their teacher preparation, they should also undergo psychoanalysis. A couch wouldn't be required, but what is needed is for them to be able to allow these residues out into the open, these signs of elitism, a profound elitism, and work for all teachers, after all, to gain a willingness to be open to popular culture.

Means to utopia
The first thing that utopians need to do, constantly, is to work for utopia to be made possible; the only way to experience utopia is by making it viable. If we don't make it viable, then it will inevitably remain utopian, in the negative sense of the expression, and not in the true sense of the word: that it is an impossible dream today that we need to render possible tomorrow. And it is in the process of this search that we need to find the means, but in order to discover and to believe in the means, once again we need knowledge, because I can't arrive at the means through pure intuition, and even when I arrive at certain means intuitively, I need that which will make me ever more critical, that will guarantee unequivocally that I learn the negotiating role of the practice in which I'm involved.

For example, when a general carries out a coup d'état, he seeks the means, do you understand? The coup doesn't happen just like that. It occurs shrouded in mediation. Sometimes this mediation is deeply personal. Nevertheless, it exists, and it is something we need in order to progress in practice, and once again I believe that when you put this idea forward, your curiosity can receive the technical denomination of epistemology, because it isn't just a curiosity about the superficiality of the object, but rather a curiosity that draws you inside the object in order to understand it and its raison d'être. It's not easy to do this. It's not easy to make politics, and this thing that we call popular education is political, it's political practice at its purest, and involves a cognitive process, a process of knowledge acquisition, finality, etc. It's political practice.

A model for an alternative society
Now we come to the discussion about the lack of alternatives nowadays, especially since the fall of the so-called socialist world. All of a sudden, the left throughout the world got a fright, the right became emboldened, secure in its neoliberal discourse. But I have no doubt whatsoever that this won't last. This discourse won't last fifteen years. Not only in Europe, but also in the United States, this discourse is starting to be contested, principally in relation to the role of the state, because one of the central arguments of this discourse is that the state should renounce everything; they have almost reached the Marxist utopia in which the state disappears, except that in this case everything must be privatized. Deep down, what the ruling class is doing is privatizing the state; the state becomes the property of the ruling class. But this neoliberal wave is turned toward Latin America and not toward the more robust systems prevailing in the United States, Germany, and Japan.

On the other hand, up until now the capitalist world has been blaming the communist world for everything. The capitalist world couldn't solve the problem of hunger within it because it had to deal with the "evils" of the communist world, but now capitalism will have to solve its problems without recourse to a scapegoat. For example, what's happening to the widely publicized excellence of capitalism? I ask myself, *What is this excellence that exists cheek by jowl with millions of people living on the streets?* As far as I'm concerned, it's enough for a man and a woman to be living homeless on the streets for me to conclude that the economy is not working. But it happens that it's not just one man and one woman—it's not two people on the streets—there are thousands of people, and they're on the streets because we are told that it's their responsibility. For this type of society creates an ideology that makes the ideologized party assume responsibility for the disasters the system creates. So, I end up on the street not because the system is bad, but because I have failed as a person. Black North American school kids don't learn good English, not because they are discriminated against and mistreated, but because "they are inferior." Where's the excellence of a system that tolerates discrimination and death? What excellence is this that allows the supreme leader of the system to refuse to sign a document in Rio de Janeiro that defended a minimum standard for dominated peoples, when they take everything that we have and then sell it as if it were bananas? And this is not because the American president is, in himself, a bad person, because each of us has his own bad qualities. But we are social and historical beings and we cannot cultivate virtues in a land without virtues.

Since we are talking of socialism, and beginning with the utopians we need to be once again, I have never encountered such a propitious moment in all our history for achieving our utopia as the present. Certainly not for me, for my generation, maybe for our grandchildren, which is wonderful because I often say that fifteen to twenty years weigh heavily in the life of a person, but twenty years in the life of Brazil or any nation are nothing. I don't live thinking only of my seventy years, but of the thousand years that Brazil will live to, the two thousand years of my country's entire history, of your country, of our countries. So, my work isn't limited to the five more years that I have, or the ten productive years that I shall live … maybe in ten years' time I shall stay at home more, assuming I'm alive, which I hope I will be. But I work, I speak, I sing, I shout, I love, I rant, I hate on behalf of the history that needs to be made in our countries, and seen from this standpoint, we have never had a better opportunity than now. As far as I can see, the mask of a whole false and falsifying ideology is being torn off. But it doesn't come off by itself; we need to smash it, by which I mean we have to work toward achieving this. And in this sense, I like the party I belong to in Brazil, the Workers' Party, that continues to say "no," that continues to refuse any type of conciliation that it considers unethical. It continues to shout, it continues to denounce President Collor. And it is no coincidence that we, in the Workers' Party, got millions of votes. Lula was almost president of the republic, and as I was on my way here, I read the results of surveys done throughout the country that showed that Lula would win an election if it were held now. How can this be explained? People know that Lula's discourse is that of a sensible socialist, a democratic socialist.

In Brazil, there are people who are scared to death of Lula because he's a worker. Yes, a worker. Lula speaks and the historic situation of Brazil changes in three months, the people take to the streets once again. This doesn't mean that President Collor should be ousted by a coup. Certainly not, because it would be a step backward for the political process of Brazil, as well as of Latin America, it would be a terrible example for the world. But even if he remains as president by means of subterfuge, the history of Brazil has changed completely in three months!

For me, one of the gravest risks is to succumb to the temptation of fatalism and immobility. It's the risk of saying, "There's nothing to be done, these people have so much power and there's nothing we can do." I believe we can do something—the very experience of a change in government. For example, we have now had a government in São Paulo for the last four years and we have managed to do things differently in those four years: we have finished with dishonesty at the highest level, we have intervened in the intermediary levels of government, but unfortunately, we haven't won the battle at the lowest levels. . . .

Some middle-ranking officers have continued to fiddle . . . but we've only had four years . . . if we had eight, we'd probably get to the root of the problem. We've brought the popular masses into the offices of the public administration to discuss the question of the city's budget with the mayor. There's no greater way of participating than this: participating in the drawing up of the public spending budget. We have transformed schools . . . in just four years. Tomorrow, a right-wing government will get voted in, it will undo 50 percent of what we did, but the day after we'll win again, and in this way, backward and forward we'll make history as continuity and above all, as possibility. History is what is possible, not what is determined.

Tolerance
My discourse is a discourse of tolerance. It's a discourse that, because it is tolerant, defends unity in diversity. This means that it is no longer possible for us to be separated here in Latin America just because it is in the interests of imperialism that we should be separated. We must overcome the power of the ruling classes who also don't want to see us united, so that they can exploit us more effectively. We must go beyond differences in order to gain, create, and invent a unity that is necessary and indispensable. I would suggest to you that unity in diversity is something that is invented politically. It doesn't exist as a spontaneous phenomenon. It exists only as a created phenomenon; it is invented and therefore a political act, an act of political decision, in which its leaders must turn it into a pedagogical object, by which I mean that they should debate what unity in diversity means with groups representing the people whenever possible.

Session Two

Second Round of Questions
A question that bothers me a lot and that concerns many people is the role of the teacher in popular education ... let's say ... the teacher's most important characteristics. There's a lot of talk about coherence, the coherence of an educator's life and also the coherence he should have, in the sense of what he ought to be. Because we can't develop a system of popular education that is devoid of commitment; its definition is that it must adopt a position. So, in adopting its position, it must necessarily be located in some place, with its own particular perspective.

Another thing that gives me some concern is the frequent debate about what the formation of a popular educator should consist of. It is logical that it is a nonacademic formation; it is necessarily a formation based on experience, but where is its point of departure and what should its end purpose be? From what perspective is this formation viewed? And something that always helps me to reflect is what a famous popular educator, Jesus Christ, once said: "Where its treasure lies, there lies its heart." And so in this sense, it seems to me that we should look at the question of coherence and what we are seeking through the act of educating. We're not serving one particular type of education or another, but we certainly are serving men and women.

It so happens that my field of activity is visual, and so I rely very much on what I can see and not only on what I can hear. What's seen remains with us; what we hear passes. I'm very scared of words. I always return to the example of the Tower of Babel and I think that in many ways, we are still in the Tower of Babel. I'd like to ask Paulo Freire to give me, rather than definitions, conceptualizations of parallel terms that are sometimes not rigidly parallel. The binaries I have in mind are education-institution, teaching-learning, content-form, and, finally—I don't see this as a binary like the other pairs—the concept of method as a model. I don't know whether I need to explain further what I mean by this aspect of "as a model." I think it might be appropriate to explain my thinking on this: you spoke about the personal appearance of the educator, the importance of this, and I noted down here, attitude and respect. It's often not necessary to display veneration in order to demonstrate respect—on the contrary—but I think it's important to consider method as a model. And so I'd like to hear your opinion on this.

Very often, what I do or what I say is not as important as how I do it or how I say it; this, for me, is the method. My field is education through art, which may seem a bit elitist, but isn't, as far as I'm concerned. It's the path ahead, which can be followed in any other educational field, because the term art, for me, doesn't have the generally accepted meaning (and that's where the Tower of Babel comes in), but it is the expression, the expression par excellence. I'd like to know

whether I'm mistaken or whether this idea, this dream, this utopia of using education through art in popular education, is a possible way ahead or not.

Paulo Freire's Answers
I'm going to try and give you my position with regard to education-institution, teaching-learning, and content-form, but I'm going to start with the last part.

I'm in complete agreement with you. But I'm so radical when it comes to the question of the understanding of education as art that I don't even use the expression you used of *education through art*, which is the title of a famous book by Herbert Read.[3] And I don't use it because, for me, education is already art, so I don't talk about education through art because it is artistic from the outset. That said, I can also understand the tacit use of the expression and I also try and enable art to serve as a vehicle for education that enhances art. For example, it was no coincidence that when I took on the role of secretary for education for São Paulo, I sought out teachers in various fields of activity from the [Pontifical] Catholic University [of São Paulo], the University of São Paulo, and the University of Campinas, and we organized workshops in the fields of linguistics, physics, mathematics, history, philosophy, and social sciences, and I managed to bring together eighty of the best teachers in the state of São Paulo. The administration continues to work with courses, groups, and review bodies through protocols that I signed with the rectors of these universities. And one of the first groups we created was devoted to art—a group of educators led by Ana Mae Barbosa, who is an expert in these matters.

So I'm in complete agreement with you, complete agreement with your interpretation about the method and the importance of the method as a creation of the educator. I'm in total agreement with this, which is why no two educators are the same. If the method or technique established by teacher A, B, or C could be experienced by all in the same way, all would be the same . . . but this is just not possible.

You observe a teacher who moves around in a particular way in the classroom, who uses her body and her language efficiently in order to communicate, using her own method. This is of incredible importance; as I often say, sometimes the most important thing is not what the educator says, but how he does what he says. So I'm in complete agreement with you.

Now, with regard to the series of apparent contradictory terms, I would say that here, they are in a dialectical relationship between different poles. For example, there is no instruction that is not educational and there's no education that is not instructive: so it is ingenuous to separate instruction from education. To say, for instance, "but he's only an instructor" is completely simplistic; and to say, "but he's more of an educator than an instructor" just doesn't bear thinking about. When you instruct, you educate; when you educate, you instruct. A great Italian educator by the name of Lombardo Radice said, "Instruction and education are the two sides of the same coin." So the educator should live dialectically between instructing and educating. This is closely related to the question of teaching and learning, because there's no teaching without learning, and no learning without teaching. Seen together, the two constitute crucial stages in a process: the process of gaining knowledge.

In this process, both are committed in their encounter with each other: on one hand, the educator, and on the other, the educatees. While the educator teaches, he learns. First of all, he learns to teach; secondly, he relearns that which he has already learned, and which he is now teaching; thirdly, he learns through the student's learning process, the person being educated; fourthly, he learns once again because he sees anew or reacquires his capacity for knowledge through the educatee's capacity for knowledge.

That's how things are in education-instruction, in teaching-learning. There are no dichotomies. There are dialectics. The same thing happens in the case of content and form. It's not possible to separate one from the other. All form has a content and all content is dressed in some form. And both have to be coherent in relation to one another. It's not possible, for example, to have progressive content dressed up in a reactionary form, and vice versa. The right never does this. What the right does very skillfully is to give a progressive *discourse* to a reactionary *practice*. It does this with good results—Collor did this with excellent results—which is, at heart, a populist approach. In his proclamations, he provided a progressive discourse in which "he would root out corruption," except that he himself was one of the "corrupt." He couldn't root himself out. The relationship between content and form is, after all, one of dialectics.

With regard to the other question, when someone asks about the profile of a popular educator, one first needs to define what type of popular educator we are talking about, because the right also has popular educators, and the profile of a progressive educator can't be the same as that of a reactionary educator, and vice versa. It is necessary to define this profile, and that's not being in any way sectarian. Sectarianism would involve denying the right-wing popular educator his right to work. The question is also contradictory, juxtaposed. A progressive educator's profile should even be demarcated by the person himself, in his practice. At the same time, there's no problem if, before embarking on his practice, he has a few ideas noted down, a few "clues" as to what this profile consists of. For example, for me, a progressive educator should be a modest person. That is, he should be open to popular truth, which may not necessarily be *his* truth. This means that the popular educator who is progressive should acknowledge and respect popular truth. To acknowledge the existence of a "popular wisdom" that has been formed in the social practice itself of which these popular groups are part. A wisdom that evolves, that takes shape whether the masses work or not. By this I mean that the fact that these popular masses are "alive" means they produce a certain culture, a certain wisdom.

The humility of the progressive educator suggests that he or she displays the necessary openness and respect to this wisdom, which often passes the progressive educator by. For example, on one occasion, an educator from São Paulo told me that in a group, a cultural circle that was dealing with the teaching of literacy, a man from the northeast of Brazil, during a discussion, referred to the question of night and day. This man gave an explanation that the whole group accepted. I'm going to repeat his beautiful explanation, which doesn't correspond to any scientific discovery. The man said, "Night is the result of the sun's batteries growing weary, when the sun is exhausted from its work during the day; and so it goes into a huge tunnel made especially for the purpose, and rests there while its batteries recharge, and when they're ready, daybreak comes and it emerges from the tunnel to light up the world." It's a beautiful story, but it's not scientific.

This is the wisdom of common sense, but there are other manifestations of common sense that are almost as rigorous as ours that are based in science. What is the role of the popular educator in the face of all this? It is to show respect and not to smile ironically on hearing this definition of the sun, the night and the day. If, on the following day, there's any interest in exploring this further, the educator can come back with a scientific argument, or even bring along an expert in physics to provide some explanation of the phenomenon.

Here's another recent case: every Tuesday, I work in Campinas with a group of scientists, physicists, mathematicians, biologists, philosophers. We call the group the "asparagus club" because we all eat asparagus. Our meetings always take place between 9 and 12:30, around a table with dishes of asparagus and a bottle of excellent *cachaça*. For more than three hours, we discuss science, epistemology, the philosophy of science, popular wisdom, the question of common sense, and so on. And in one of these meetings, a biologist (one of those people who work a lot with Indians) told us that a young lad, a big strong adolescent, had told him, "Look, tomorrow I'm going to teach you how to fish with a harpoon." So the scientist, who was curious, and didn't want to pass up an opportunity to learn how the Indian did this, said, "Okay, let's go." The following morning, they set off really early in a canoe and immediately a beautiful fish appeared and so the boy told the scientist, "Look, and see how I catch it." The scientist saw that the boy didn't throw the harpoon straight at the fish, but between the fish and the canoe … and he caught it. He pulled the fish out of the water and the scientist understood what had happened, but he wanted to make sure how he knew, and so he said, "Look, I don't understand; you didn't throw the harpoon at the fish, but between the fish and the canoe. Why was that?" And the boy replied, "I threw the harpoon at the fish, but your eyes were deluded. It was an optical illusion."

Refraction, for the Indians, is a question of the eyes being deluded. For us, it's refraction, do you see? Now, I ask myself: what should we do with what the Indian said at that moment? Say, "No, it has nothing to do with the eyes being deluded. It's a physical phenomenon that we whites have long called refraction of light, and so on and so forth"? No! If the economic conditions of that community change, if they undergo a process of modernization, whether capitalist or socialist, then in either of these scenarios, there will be a need to go beyond the interpretation of "optical illusion."

These are the virtues of humility, of the capacity to be open to popular culture, to popular understanding, to the magical understanding of the world. They are qualities that popular educators must foster if they are progressive, but if they are of the right, then the opposite occurs.

Another quality I see is the ability to take things seriously, the respect shown in the way one shows popular groups how to work, how to do things. That's why, for example, I've never accepted that a young middle-class boy or girl, who is used to wearing branded trainers, should discard these just because they are going to a proletarian area and want to show that they're "poor." No, this is wrong. Proletarian people know it's a lie because they can guess, they know even by the "smell," that the person is from outside. So it's a lie and one doesn't change the world by lying. We need to take things seriously, honestly.

Another quality is not being ashamed to say when one is tired. That's why I want to, and indeed should tell you: I'm tired.

Popular Education in Paraguay: Our Questions to Freire

[Based on individual questions jotted down on bits of paper, themes were grouped together and listed in the order below, so that they could be put to Paulo later in the seminar.]

1. Popular education: the inclusion of intellectuals in this process. Women: the issues of gender. Children in popular education.

2. Effects of and changes achieved by popular education in the formation, development, and consolidation of popular organizations in Latin America.

3. The intentionality of popular education and its method of assessment using verifiable indicators: the problem of assistencialism and autosuggestion.

4. The educator: his/her power, limitations, charisma, leadership, impatience.

5. Popular education: culture. Cultural heritage. The problem of cultural history. Identity and cultural resistance.

6. Relationship among educator-base-organization-people.

7. Popular political education: party politics, organization, the problem of power. The autonomy of popular education. To what extent popular education has any autonomy.

8. Methodological aspects: popular education and formal education—popular education's possible inclusion in official education. The transformation from instinctive awareness to critical awareness and commitment to change.

9. Popular education and the rhythm of history: the link between the struggle for economic-pay-productive rights and a process of libertarian education. The technical and scientific avalanche in the development of popular education.
10. Regarding Brazilian reality: the contribution of the churches in the formation of class awareness in Brazil. The development of organizations and class consciousness in Brazil.
11. Some solutions emerging from popular education for the neoliberal onslaught in Latin America.[4]

Faced with these themes, my initial reaction is that they are like the index of a book that I couldn't write. I think it's complex, but it's a book we could write together.[5]

Item 1: Popular education: the inclusion of intellectuals in this process. Women: the issues of gender. Children in popular education.
It's obvious that in popular education, even from a reactionary, conservative perspective, there's probably also a concern for these elements or components, but with a focus on how to make use of intellectuals in order to go on deceiving the public more efficiently. And it's possible that there's a concern for working with women, but also in the sense of duping them. I believe that this is a delicate subject, because it's one of the positions in which many of us, progressive men, contradict ourselves: our discourse is progressive. We speak out against exploitation, and yet we are sexist. I think this is awful. The fact is that I know a lot of revolutionary folks who are different when they are at home and try to manipulate their women-folk's future. Of course, women have been fighting for their rights for years, and they are more independent, but there are huge contradictions, even in the use of language. Our language is still one rooted in "macho" attitudes, and we say it's a question of "syntax," a question of grammar, but it isn't that at all. For example, how can we explain that in a place like

this, with a large number of people—let us suppose that there is only one man and the rest are women, why is it that I have to address you in the masculine form? Why? Please don't tell me that it's because when there is one man and one woman, the masculine form of address has to be used. Why "*todos*" [masculine] and not "*todas*" [feminine]? Who established this rule? There's only one explanation: it's a sexist ideology that manifests itself in a nonneutral way through language. So, we need to revolutionize language as well. This means that if we seek to bring about change in the world, we've got to reinvent language so that it is no longer sexist. And what is incredible is that women assimilate this. They are invaded by the language of male dominance and obey it; they also address a whole crowd using the masculine form, even if there's only one man. If I were to address you all as "*todas*," using the feminine form, the man among you would be annoyed with me or would think that I am ignorant in matters of syntax. . . . In this latest book of mine, *Pedagogy of Hope*, I devote an entire section to this question because the language used in *Pedagogy of the Oppressed* is a language riddled with male sexism. When the book came out in the 1970s, I began to get letters from women in the United States praising it, but saying, "You are contradictory; you said at one point in your book, 'I believe in the capacity of men to change the world,' but why not women, as well?" And I remember that when I read the first letters, I said to my first wife, "My God, when I say man I include woman, as well!" This is the deceitful, ideological explanation, with which all children learn and develop, because if I were to say, "Women will one day transform the world," no man would feel himself to be included. Now, who decided that when I say "man," woman is included? Men invented this.

Language, my friends, is ideological. We need to be aware, to feel, to understand that language is not neutral, but ideological. It's permeated with ideology. One hears so many conversations, for example, like this one: "Do you know Maria?" and the other person says, "Ah! Yes, I know her, she's . . . (and the person hesitates, without knowing how to continue) . . . a black girl, but excellent." And why the "but"? I've never heard anyone say, "She's a blonde, blue-eyed girl, but she's excellent." But when referring to a black girl, the "but" sounds perfectly natural. Precisely because "but" is an adversarial conjunction—that is, a conjunction that joins a statement that in large measure contradicts the other. In other words, it's as if being black means you can't be excellent. So what's this all about? It's an ideological language that's used in relation to Indians, blacks, women, everything.

I see one of the first concerns of intellectuals in progressive popular education as being to look closely at themselves before anything else, to see to their own conversion. One needs to go through a process of conversion, and it's not easy. The sexist imprint is very deep in us. Our *machismo* is deeply ingrained in us, and it's not easy to overcome this. And what's worse is that it's not enough to overcome *machismo* in our discourse. For example, I know many men who don't make the bed where they sleep with their wife because that's a woman's task. Why is it only the woman who makes the bed where they have made love? Why, if it's so easy for men? I know men who can't even clear the plates from the table. Only a few are capable of serving wine or some other drink to friends they have invited to dinner in their home, but the woman does everything, and when it's not his wife then it's a woman who is badly paid, exploited, and who is in his house as a domestic servant. I don't want to give the impression that I'm a priest; only yesterday a young woman joked with me and asked me when I'd left the cloth, and I said, "I never even went to the seminary!"

I don't want to give a sermon, a speech of a religious character, but it's true, it's a question of coherence. We talked this morning about the need to be consistent, to strive for consistency between word and action, and I acknowledge that this is one of the most difficult aspects. I remember, for example, that when I was in Geneva, I received the first letters from North American women, and after the fourth, I thought, *What they're saying to me is right; it's not true that when I say "men" I'm including women.* So then I replied to each one and embarked on a new stage in my life. This was at the beginning of 1971.

I remember that one of the first things I did was to speak to my two sons, who were adolescents, and I said to them, "Look, we are three men and we're exploiting the women of the house. One of them is my wife and your mother, and the others are your sisters and my daughters, and I don't think we can go on like this," to which I added, "Look, boys, we don't tidy the house we're living in, you don't make your beds and I don't make the bed in which my wife and I sleep" (it was my first wife). Another thing I'd like to say is that one of my failures was that I never learned to cook, but I never learned not because I didn't want to ideologically, but because I was scared. I should have had some counseling, but now, I don't need to anymore because I know what the problem is. It's because deep down, women themselves (I don't know whether it's the same in Paraguay) identify the kitchen with femininity. And this is the ideology that the male has planted in the woman's head: a man who cooks is effeminate and the woman says, "Men aren't allowed in the kitchen"—see what an easy life men have! But now, things are different: a girl insists on a degree of equality in relation to the boy right from the start, and he either accepts this or has to get out—there's no other option. There have been such radical changes in this matter that it's sometimes difficult to recognize them. My generation wasn't like this and it was difficult for me to adjust not only my language, but also various other things. I confess that if I could cook, it would be a big step forward. All I can do is to fry eggs very well, I can make good juices, I can prepare drinks, I know how to make the bed very well, I lay the table, I serve. I know how to do all this. I even wash the dishes that we've used at dinner, but now Nita has bought a dishwasher and left me at a loss: I can't do the dishes anymore. Now, you may say to me, "For God's sake, Paulo, here we are in Paraguay, which is exploited, and in Brazil, which is plunged into poverty, and all you can talk about is women and sexist language. We'd do better to change the world first and then deal with these things." But I say to you, no, changing our language is part of changing the world, changing our culture is part of changing the world, and we shouldn't wait to do so. It's through exercises such as this, which are almost always painful, that we also develop in ourselves.

To sum up, it's a basic premise for a progressive popular educator, because if I use what is fundamentally sexist language, then I probably hold women in lesser esteem or tend to consider them less able than myself. How can I be an educator for liberation if my basic principle is that women are a "little bit" inferior to me? We can't ignore this aspect.

But there are other aspects that seem to be more closely linked to the questions we are debating. For example, one of these could be the task of the intellectual in the field of popular education. What to do if I'm a philosopher? What can I contribute to the field of popular education without ceasing to be a philosopher? If I'm a mathematician, for example, if I'm a biologist, a historian, or a grammar teacher, what can I do? There are thousands of things I can do, but the first things a progressive intellectual has to do in relation to his experience of knowledge correspond closely to what he has to do in relation to his experience of knowledge about sexuality. In the same way that this hypothetical intellectual has to ask himself about his relationship with and perception of the role of women, he also has to ask himself about his role as an intellectual and academic. He has to extricate himself from this terrible ideology, which is precisely the ideology of academicians, and is at heart elitist, corresponding as it does to the interests of an elite that this intellectual represents. In this way, he should ask himself if he is able to consider himself an intellectual serving the popular classes rather than just serving his students in their curiosity to learn. If he is capable of contributing to the popular struggle rather than merely accompanying their reading of texts by Hegel and Marx. . . . It's far worse to only know how to discuss Marx in book form rather than to understand Marx in the struggle on the streets. This seems more tragic to me than dramatic.

The same thing happens in the case of the female intellectual. She also has to analyze her relations and her role, whether she exaggerates or not in her struggle for her identity as a woman, whether or not she likes male sexist language, whether she agrees or not with her husband's never making the bed, not even on Sunday, because he has reading and writing to do. Because this was the argument I used; I never did any housework because if I did, I wouldn't write. Yet my first wife, before we went into exile, did both things: she worked in school and worked at home with the children, looked after the home and cooked, and she could do all these things. But, as a man, I could only think of these tasks as being a woman's job. It was incredible, just incredible. A woman has got to ask herself whether she can go on like this. Look, I'm not suggesting that women should start asking for divorce, no. There are marriages that last for many years within these parameters.... But what I do say is that women have a duty to fight for their rights. I must confess that I can't understand, I just can't understand how a woman can fight for the liberation of peasants, but not for her own liberation. And I can see a contradiction here, which is why we must be radical. But this doesn't mean that a woman should leave her husband, go on strike in matters of sex....

I was saying that if the intellectual is a woman, she needs to ask herself what she can do, what her contribution should be, for example, as a mathematician, at the present time in Brazil, and probably in Paraguay as well. I'm not acquainted with academic life in Paraguay, but in Brazil at the moment one often hears that scientists are devoting themselves to "ethnoscience." These scientists, with whom I meet up every Tuesday, are involved in the following: apart from giving classes in physics, in astronomy in university postgraduate courses, they debate with the people, do research into their different levels of knowledge, how the people acquire this knowledge, and what they know. There are many contributions that intellectuals can make in this area. You, for example, have a right to say to the members of your team, "I don't want to go out into the countryside, I don't want to go into areas where people are suffering, I want to work on the 'theory of educational practice.'" There's no reason why that preference can't be catered to. From time to time, we can invite an educator who has been out in the country to give us a report, during the course of a morning, on his experience of rural-dwellers, so that he can give us his scientific interpretation of the behavior of peasants in various types of situation. In this way, both educators and peasants can contribute in their own way.

No opportunity should be lost to contribute to the struggle, but at the same time one should never dictate what has to be done. This was one of the mistakes of Stalinism, and in Brazil there's a very clear example of this: you know the architect Oscar Niemeyer.... It's said that when he was a militant in the Communist Party and a member of the PCB [Brazilian Communist Party] youth, when he was already famous but still young, he received an order to go and join the party militants on the streets to paint slogans along the walls, at a time when the police were clamping down very harshly on this, and this order was given so that he wouldn't remain an intellectual far removed from the people. This was ridiculous. Because, in making Niemeyer do this, valuable time was wasted when he could have been giving people the benefit of his reflection, and they didn't even get a good graffiti artist. This was just moronic, stupid.

I believe we need to pay close attention to the specific qualities of intellectuals in a process of popular education; we need to make good use of the special knowledge that each one possesses, and of what they can and may want to achieve. For example, we need to ask mathematicians, "Come with us on Saturday to see how the poor kids sell things and how they do their addition without any knowledge of so-called official math." Study proposals to see how we can improve the teaching of arithmetic and other branches of mathematics in marginalized areas.

If you're a mathematician or a biologist, you shouldn't be satisfied with only the classes you give at the university. Any specialization can be important for supporting popular education, for reaching a more humanistic and more scientific understanding of the cultural identity of the people. For example, many teachers acted without any respect at all for the children of the lower classes, convinced that all knowledge is acquired exclusively in school, but children don't need to go to school to gain knowledge—they need school to learn how to use their knowledge better. Now, for children to learn how to use their knowledge through school, the school needs to be scientifically, lovingly, pedagogically prepared for such a task. So this could be the subject of group workshops for those involved in popular education.

On the other hand, I think union activity needs to be directed beyond things like pay negotiations, which are, of course, necessary—very important and necessary—but they also need to think about improving conditions for teaching. Above all, they need to think about the political and pedagogical project of popular education.

Item 2: Effects of and changes achieved by popular education in the formation, development, and consolidation of popular organizations in Latin America.
There's no doubt that in Paraguay, Brazil, or Argentina—it doesn't matter where—and with all the experience we have accumulated in popular education in Latin America, practices have differed depending on the different historical contexts. In some areas, these differences were more pronounced, in others less so, in some our experiences were easier, in others more difficult.

It was one thing to embark on popular education five years ago, and it was another to do so fifteen years ago. Fifteen years ago was far more difficult than five years ago. Five years ago, the dictatorship was probably changing because "it was growing exhausted" and it therefore relaxed a little "while it was taking a siesta," and you started popular education while the dictatorship was taking a siesta. Nowadays, much more can be done. It's possible to challenge the government itself without fear of immediate arrest, so that the limits of what one can do have been expanded to embrace all practical areas. In Brazil, for example, how did we manage to carry out popular education during the long period of military dictatorship? It was extraordinarily difficult, but we did it nevertheless. In a big country, a really big country, we managed to do it in many places, clandestinely, without anybody knowing.

The CEBs [Ecclesiastical Base Communities], which constituted an exceptional launchpad for struggle, were turned into extraordinary centers for popular education, where an understanding of the relationship between material and transcendental reality constituted a crucial and basic point of departure.

So, faced with this, I am convinced that if we make a real effort in popular education, we shall have an effect and achieve change. Now, what changes might these be? We don't know, because that is a task for historians. We would need a historical analysis in order to know what happened in Paraguay and to know what is happening now in relation to the activities of popular education for the formation, development, and consolidation of popular organizations. I believe there's a thesis concealed in all this and that may be translated into a question: is it possible for popular education to help in the consolidation of popular organizations? I say it is possible. It will depend on how we work; it will depend on our lucidity, on the political clarity of our thought, and it will also depend on our scientific formation.

I would now like to make a comment that is related to all this. I don't know whether you have experienced the same phenomenon as the one I'm about to tell you. In Brazil, one often hears the argument that denies the value of the university or academia because one considers it bourgeois, the knowledge it propounds overly ornate and vacuous, but if one denies academia, one also denies the value of theory. Such a position argues that practice alone is valid, and a number of meetings were held in Brazil with respect to this, during which it was made clear that only people with practical experience could speak there; those who only think from a purely academic perspective have no right to speak. In the first place, this is authoritarian; it's not democratic. Secondly, it's extremely stupid; it has no scientific basis whatsoever. The other position reflects the complete opposite of this: that only academia has any value; only theory has any value; practice makes no sense at all. Well, the first constitutes an ideological deviance to which we attribute the term *grassrootism*: knowledge is the preserve of the grassroots, only the grassroots are virtuous. The Church fell very much for this discourse and the ultra-revolutionaries identified themselves with a "religion" that was "the religion of the grassroots." Only the grassroots know, only the grassroots are virtuous; it is all about a knowledge that is independent, self-contained, and doesn't need the theoretical knowledge of academics. The other position is what we call *elitism*, which completely denies the importance of practical experience; it is enough for someone to develop an elegant, theoretical discourse for the world to be saved.

In this matter, I'm convinced that both positions work against change. They are both reactionary: the cult of the grassroots is as reactionary as elitism. One presents us with a reactionary attitude among the people, while the other, elitism, reflects a reactionary position that is far removed from the people. The true position of people who are committed to real, progressive popular education is that which views the relationship between theory and practice dialectically, because at heart these two positions are intertwined in a dialectical or non-dialectical understanding of the relationship between theory and practice, which was so dear to Marx. That is, there is no theory that doesn't need to be practically proved. It's the practice that tells me whether a theory is correct. But, by the same token, there's no practice that doesn't contain within it a degree of theory.

This being the case, for me, the formation of a teacher, the formation, for example, of agents of popular education—who do not need to be university academics—as well as the political and scientific formation of young male and female popular educators must be carried out by reflecting critically on the practical experience that a person has, by which I mean, by analyzing the practical experience that you yourself and others possess and the theory that underpins it. But theory should not negate practice, nor should practice negate theory. This would constitute a terrible mistake.

Item 3: The intentionality of popular education and its method of assessment using verifiable indicators: the problem of assistencialism and autosuggestion.
The third block of questions speaks of the intentionality of popular education in its method of assessment using verifiable indicators; voluntary assistance provision versus autonomous self-management. The dialectical question of the relationship between theory and practice permeates all this, given that the two constitute, in their process, one contradictory, dialectical whole, which cannot conceivably be broken.

It is difficult to understand this process. I believe we have to pay it particular attention, even if we conclude that, at heart, the provision of assistance is a type of authoritarianism with a sugar coating. Fundamentally, this type of assistance hinders the capacity of the people to make decisions. Populism gives popular classes the illusion that they have autonomy—they think they are acting, when in fact they're being used; they're not acting at all. The assistance-providing leadership acts through the "assisted," who is given the impression that he or she has gained independence and freedom. Of course, this isn't one of progressive popular education's blatant contradictions, but applies more to reactionary popular education.

We should take great care to specify very precisely what we mean by self-management. Its purpose is to assume freedom and creativity, which seems excellent to me. The only problem is that I am sometimes scared by certain self-management experiences that, in their idealistic assumptions, deny the need for any type of external intervention. I must confess to you that my conception of democracy doesn't deny the role of democratic leadership. I continue to believe in the need for democratic leadership, which is why I defend the existence of teachers. How, for instance, could one envisage a teacher who doesn't lead? How could one envisage a teacher who doesn't teach? The fact of teaching, the fact of contributing directly to the formation of one's students, involves assuming leadership. I criticize the authoritarian form of leadership. Self-management, in effect, leads to the emergence of small groups of leaders, because one doesn't lead through metaphysical self-management; in the process of self-management there are those individuals who administer, who, in effect, do the managing.

Item 4: The educator: his/her power, limitations, charisma, leadership, impatience.
The fourth block is about the educator and his or her power, limitations, charisma, leadership, and impatience. I believe the educator has all these things; the question is to live them and put them into practice in a coherent way. That the educator has a certain degree of power is undeniable. This power lies precisely in the power of his knowledge, which is sometimes an assumed knowledge, but that doesn't matter. He or she has a certain power that is rooted in the fact that he or she knows something. That's why I think that for him or her to be able to justify correctly his power, he or she must prepare himself or herself permanently, his or her process of formation must be continuous. Now, observe how this question is a vicious circle. Sometimes, educators earn so little that they are scared of protesting, of pursuing their demands, and they can end up by being stifled by their fear and lack of preparation. And the greater their fear and lack of preparation, the less likely they are to communicate to their students their own need to fight for their liberation. This circle has to be broken, and the decision to do this must come from progressive governments.

You are currently preparing for presidential elections and we must be on our guard: to know whom to vote for, whom to fight for in order to be elected, which is the best candidate. And you must also make your expectations felt. You can't adopt the puritanical position of "this isn't a question I want to get involved in." A government that calls itself progressive must insist on breaking the circle a little, and it must also challenge teachers and educators. Power exists, but it must be used well. There are limits to it, as well, because an educator can't do everything. The power of a popular educator is a power that is already born with limitations because its practice is limited. His or her limitations are political, economic, and social; historical, ideological, and scientific insofar as his or her competence is concerned.

So in this way, one of the things that educators need to know is that their practice has its limitations. The educator can't do everything, but he or she can do something. Given today's historical conditions, what is historically possible? What is it historically possible to achieve? And have no doubt, this task is also one for intellectuals. Have no doubt either that this probably doesn't feature in any academic program of political philosophy, sociology, or philosophy of education; no professor is interested in knowing what is historically possible in his country. And if you ask a famous professor, "What is historically possible in the current climate?" he or she will answer, "That's not part of my program." But this is part of his or her program; it's part of his or her country's wider program, because his or her country's program, his or her country's history, is far greater than his or her little semester "program" in his or her university.

We need to discuss these things, even with the rural folks, and while we are talking to the peasants, why not also to the men and women of the *favelas*[6] so that they too can mobilize themselves, and move into positions in which all these matters can be rethought? We should understand that this is not the exclusive preserve of half a dozen intellectual soothsayers; by this I mean that it must be of concern to society as a whole, and not just a few privileged individuals.

[Interval for participants to ask further questions.[7]]

Item 5: With regard to the question that was asked about the contribution to and participation of women in popular education, how could we reinforce the methodology used on behalf of feminism, given that this is more widely known among city-based women and doesn't reach women everywhere?
The problem is this: women make a mistake (not all women, only some) in their struggle on behalf of feminism, in the way it is generally defended. In the United States I discussed this issue a lot and sometimes women began to have doubts. They veer away from debates about sex, preferring to talk about gender. But why not talk about sex? It's much better. They take the problem of social class out of the debate about sex, and I include it. My position is this: I don't see how we can reduce the debate about sex and the debate about race to that about social classes. I just can't. But neither can I understand a debate about sex and class, or sex and race, without an understanding of class. I cannot reduce or explain sexual discrimination through an analysis of class. Secondly, I cannot explain racial discrimination through class. But I can't understand racism or sexism without analyzing social class. In this way, when a discussion about sex and race is seen in isolation, far removed from the question of social class, the outcome is that the theme of the discussion is of no interest, for example, to peasant women (a woman who quarrels with her husband because she didn't make the bed doesn't have much to do with the daily life of a peasant woman); and yet a peasant woman is as much an object, if not more so, than a woman of the bourgeoisie. When it comes down to it, the bourgeois woman passes the responsibility on to the maids, because she pays them and she has other compensations; she can dress well, she may be the center of attention, she has a right to satisfy her whims. It is hard for a peasant woman to have dreams, but women of the bourgeoisie can dream about whomever they want. Her husband isn't aware, and she doesn't need psychotherapy because of it. . . .

For this reason, we need to take this debate to women of the popular classes (using all the appropriate tactics, of course), because if we introduce the theme of machismo to a group of peasant women, then their husbands will probably stop them from joining any more meetings, and all our hard work will have been in vain. If the strategy is to contribute a little, whatever we can, to change the world, then I must make a concession. Politics aren't possible without concessions, but there are limits to what one might concede. So, in order not to risk the women not coming back to meetings, it's better not to begin by talking about machismo, and let the theme emerge naturally in the course of time.

Item 6: I and many of my fellow countrymen are worried that a theme that proved useful in creating awareness may become the preserve of elites as it passes from a popular-based knowledge to an academic one, that it will become a knowledge based in universities and therefore lose the inner quality that was responsible for the genesis of all this, and that was based in the knowledge of the people. What can we do to ensure that the people don't lose the ownership, the essence behind the practice of popular education?
My understanding is that we've got a political question here that, because it is political, involves first and foremost a question of the power of the popular group and the power of the educators who are working with popular groups. Secondly, it involves a question of tactics and consciousness, in respect to which you are right. The problem you mention is not that the intellectuals A, B, or C, may take possession of the results elaborated by the popular groups, distance themselves from them, or negate them, etc. The problem is that the educators and the people need to go beyond a type of knowledge that we recognize as starting from the premise "I think it is" and achieve a knowledge that enables us to be aware of the raison d'être of the object, the raison d'être of reality. In other words, we urgently need to reach beyond a knowledge that only limits itself to experience and seek a greater scientific rigor.

Academics are supposed to have a greater talent for exactness, although many don't because they were appointed not because they were good teachers, committed to popular causes, but because they were important lawyers, famous doctors, etc.

To sum up, what I defend is not the separation between one knowledge and another, nor do I argue that popular knowledge is inferior. What I do argue is that in order to progress further, we undoubtedly need a more elaborate patrimony geared toward a more exact form of knowledge. Now, this will depend on the power base that we ourselves build, on the political power, so that we can encourage intellectuals to join us, because it's not any university intellectual who will come to us, given that some are unable to rid themselves of their elitist posture. It is our responsibility to say to them, "Look, we need you, but not just this—we need your knowledge, which we respect, but we want you to respect the knowledge of the people." The question is how to create a dialogue, how to suggest a dialogue between popular knowledge and the so-called scientific-academic knowledge, in order not to create a dichotomy.

Item 7: Paulo, you are suggesting that popular education expects the educator to be in effect a militant, the bearer of a testimony. This means that popular education would involve a new form of militancy, independent of parties or organizations. Based on this assumption, my question is the following: how far should this autonomy in education go in relation to the political process, to the organic processes and the processes of struggle that emerge from these instances that are also present in civil society? In fact, herein lies the tragedy of the intellectual who seeks to be independent of parties, apolitical, and who seeks to follow this path, sometimes in the widest sense. I would like you to give us some ideas with regard to this.

This is what I believe: firstly, a party can embark on a program of popular education; why not? What allows us to say that it can't carry out popular education just because it's a party? It won't carry out popular education not because it's a party, but because, as a party, its ideological priorities may not coincide with those supporting education for the masses. A Stalinist doesn't do popular education; a Stalinist party does popular instruction, not education. So the issue of not doing popular education doesn't belong to it as a party, but rather as an ideology, an authoritarian ideology that negates the people. Secondly, a group of intellectuals can provide popular education outside the strict physical limits of political parties. You have the example of Decidamos [Let us decide],[8] which works with any party, without any interference from their ideologies, and without the party members being necessarily neutral.

Your experience is neither exportable nor importable: I always say that experience isn't exported, but re-created. Your experience, therefore, cannot be exported—firstly because it's an experience, and secondly because experiences can't be exported. During this process of transition in Paraguay, a transition that has probably caused less suffering than the transition in Brazil, and far less suffering than the Argentinian transition, probably one of the least painful processes of transition that we are experiencing in Latin America, it is perfectly possible to work with political parties. But I don't know how long this will last; there may come a moment when the parties of the right say, "No, no, no, no! We're not interested in any more agreements with you people.…" Be in no doubt, that day will come, and the social reality of the time will tell you that you should opt for party A, B, or C.

That's why I'm not dogmatic; because a dogmatic person cannot understand history from a dogmatic point of view. For example, if people in Brazil were to ask whether I believe in the possibility of understanding history dogmatically, I would say, "I respect it, but I don't believe it." Now, in Brazil, some interesting things have been happening. Two months ago, for instance, I got a phone call from the secretary of an important "postmodern impresario" asking me to receive him along with two directors of his company. I selected a day, and they turned up at our house, mine and Nita's, and the young industrialist said to me, "Look, Professor Freire, when I was a child, an adolescent, my father, my mother, prohibited your name from being mentioned at home. Today, I'm the managing director of a company and I'm here precisely to ask you to help us better educate our workers." Do you understand? What happened was that I hadn't changed, but history had caused him to change; I continue to defend the same education that I've always supported, and he was aware of that. Now, as an intelligent man, he also knows that education has its limitations and that they were far, far behind, almost on the edge, and they realized that they could quite easily move forward ten kilometers without running any risk. Probably, when they reach the tenth kilometer, they'll stop and tell their descendants about Paulo Freire, "Look, it's not enough!" Which means that these things occur in history, and that's why you can't be deterministic; you can't see things mechanically; you can't say, "No, this can't be done, this can't happen," because maybe it will happen, when you least expect it.

At the present time, you are probably able to do innovative, transformative things, but some time from now, you won't be able to. In another society, you might not be able to do what you are able to do today. And so, my suggestion is this: make the most of these limited opportunities and do your best in the work you're doing now, and continue to do it.

The concept of autonomy is very relative, so relative that we are never completely autonomous. Let us suppose, for example, that there's a group called Cultural Action. It's an honest, serious group, but it needs funds in order to carry out its work, because although it can count on volunteers, work should be paid; otherwise the number of volunteers will decrease by the day. So, it manages to get some support from European foundations. At this point, its autonomy is put at risk. And I say this not because I've had any experiences in which organizations have tried to condition me.[9] No, this has never happened to me, and they've always treated me with respect. But what may happen is that the group is a bit inhibited, and may produce a report more to satisfy Holland than to state the truth.

In other words, we need to make the following absolutely clear: from this point on, from this nucleus, we shall make no concessions; we would rather close down our organization than make concessions, and then we shall be autonomous. That's what autonomy is as far as I'm concerned. But this doesn't mean you can't work with a progressive sector within the state. Why not? In Brazil, for example, I'm respected by various tendencies within political parties, I'm atypical, I have a certain projection; mine is invariably a political presence. Even so, I could never accept a position as an advisor to the government of President Collor, never. I could never entertain such a thought.

The struggle for political autonomy exists; there's no doubt about that. For example, when I assumed the role of secretary for education in São Paulo, I got a phone call within a week from the World Bank, which was negotiating with various institutions in the state of São Paulo. But as the capital of São Paulo "is a state," "is a country," they wanted to try and get the state and the capital together. They phoned me from Boston and arranged for an interview. I and my team received a delegation from the World Bank, we held talks, and the president of the delegation from the bank said, "Look, professor, we've got fifty million dollars to lend you, to lend the Secretariat for Education," and he added, "Now, there are one or two conditions, the first of which is that you should have fifty million as collateral." I agreed. "The second"—he continued—"is that you should hand your fifty million over to certain nongovernmental organizations" (you can imagine how nongovernmental organizations are of special interest to the neoliberals), "you hand the fifty million over to the non-governmental organizations, they don't pay off the loan, but you pay us." "Third," he said, "we lend the money for a certain type of work . . . for schools. Fourth, the female educators who will go and work for nongovernmental organizations should mainly be people without degrees or diplomas."

So I said, "Look, do you realize that 70 percent of the women teachers in the São Paulo municipal schools network have postgraduate qualifications and of the remaining 30 percent, 20 percent have university degrees and the other 10 percent have diplomas?! And you are proposing, at the very time when I am committed to a project of immense importance, costing millions of dollars to put into effect, that I should be responsible for the permanent formation of these people? Is that what you are proposing?"

Then I continued, "Look, sir, this isn't the sort of thing you propose, even in the poorest areas of the Northeast, where there's a shortage of qualified teachers. But now, I'd like to ask you a question. Let us imagine that you have asked me for something I haven't asked you for: a loan. Now let us suppose that you have asked me for 5,000 dollars (that's my limit), and that you prove to me, you demonstrate that you can pay it back. Would you find it acceptable for me to say, 'Very well, I'll lend you five thousand dollars, but there are some conditions attached: firstly, with these 5,000 dollars you've got to buy a thousand pairs of shorts made in São Paulo: 200 blue ones, 300 with printed patterns . . . and you've also got to buy a thousand ties made in Recife. . . .'" And so I presented him with a whole list of demands before agreeing to lend him the 5,000 dollars, after which I asked him, "Would you find this acceptable?" He shook his head. So I replied, "How do you think that I, who have spent time in prison, who have been expelled from my country, and who wrote a book called *Pedagogy of the Oppressed*, can accept this? Do you think I don't respect my people? No, my answer is no. . . . Thank you very much; I don't want your loan." So he said, "On what condition would you accept it?" I said there were two conditions: the first is that I shall never have to repay the loan, and the second is that I do what I want with it, without having to provide anyone with explanations or reports. These are the two assurances I need, without which, thank you very much, I don't want your money."

Then, to cap it all, he asked me, "And what if the mayor, Luiza Erundina, accepts?" I replied, "Look, there's no such thing as 'yes' in this matter. Do you know why Erundina invited me to be secretary? Because she knew, before she even made the invitation, that one day a proposal such as this one would be turned down by me. That's why she invited me, because she knew I would say 'no' to you or anyone else if I were presented with this type of proposal. But let us suppose that Erundina had gone mad and said she would accept. I would resign immediately and give an interview in which I would say Erundina has gone mad." I got up and he left along with his team. This is what we must do. This is the demonstration of dignity that we must make in the name of our people, and not just ourselves as individuals. I wouldn't have been myself if I had spoken in an overly diplomatic way.... I'm not stupid; I'm energetic, but I had a huge responsibility as the municipal secretary for education in a city like São Paulo, a huge political responsibility, both for myself and for the people, and I just had to say *no* to this, because it is just not the type of proposal that should be made.

And so in this way, I fought for our autonomy. Political lucidity tells us that when our autonomy is in danger, when it might damage the interests of the people, then we must say *no*. But if the circumstances are different, then there's no reason not to accept. If the foreigner came to me and said, "I'm giving you fifty million and I won't be seeking repayment," then money has no nationality and I would accept it and make very good use of it.

Item 8: Methodological aspects: popular education and formal education—popular education's possible inclusion in official education. The transformation from instinctive awareness to critical awareness and commitment to change. In answer to the question about whether popular education can be carried out in state schools, I would say that popular education is not merely the preserve of activities independent of the state sector. Nowadays, neoliberal discourse is using this argument and even attracting progressive people so that, for example, the state can free itself from the responsibility of providing education. I've got friends in Brazil who, five years ago, would proclaim loudly that there should be no private schools and I would say, "No, the parents have a right," and now they've gone to the other extreme and say, "All schools should be private and the state should pay the parents to educate their children." I can imagine parents queuing up for this. And how would resources be distributed? In community schools, someone would meet with thirty pupils and the following day, they'd go to the government and say, "Look, I've got a classroom that holds thirty kids," so would the state hand over the money just like that? Are you kidding? No, out of the question. So, is it possible to provide popular education in state schools? It is. Over a period of four years, we provided the highest standards of popular education in the schools of the São Paulo municipality. The issue, as far as I am concerned, is the level of political clarity among those in positions of leadership, the political coherence that we defend, and the knowledge of what is possible historically, or rather, what is possible to do now, historically, in order that we can achieve tomorrow what we were unable to achieve today.

Item 9: Some tentative solutions for this situation, from popular education to neoliberal policies in Latin America, and its overall effect on our countries.
It is my firm belief—and I insist that I may be completely wrong—that neoliberal discourse won't last for long. A year ago, I could see that wherever there was an election, in any country in the world, progressive candidates were being defeated. Now I believe there's change in the air, and as I said yesterday, I was reading the paper on my way here, and if the Brazilian presidential election were taking place today (September 1992), Lula would win. Lula is the same as ever and would beat Collor by three million votes. I'm convinced that, in all probability, he won't win in two or three years' time, but I must insist on what I said before: the life of a country,

of a nation, of a people, isn't exhausted in twenty years, or in forty or fifty years, and you know that very well … and this is a marvelous thing, because it suggests we need to show a certain humility.

When someone works because he or she enjoys it, because he or she wants to get down to achieving some results, he or she has to be prepared for the fact that it's not always possible to achieve those results.

The fact that we can't see those results in Paraguay, in Brazil, or the rest of the world, doesn't make me a pessimist or make me give up the struggle. Because what is important is not merely that I should achieve those results, but that other people, other Paulos, other Marias, other folk. And I believe that history will change soon, very soon. But I will not be here to see it. This is an expression that I've never used, but that I must say at this point: "The young people now should take up the struggle," because I'm young, too, and as a young person, I've got to fight. And I have no doubt that before long, they, too, will continue this debate themselves.

We need to work; it's crucial that we make a start. For example, that we choose a group that starts by picking out passages from neoliberal speeches that promise, that state that there are no longer any social classes, and that everything is harmonious. Let them choose them, keep them, note the date, the name of the paper, the name of the author, and let them start by reading these speeches in the group meetings: "Look, So-and-So, the candidate for Such-and-Such, said this: can it be true, that all the men and women in the world are equal?," for example. In the first place, when they start doing this, they can expect a reaction from the neoliberals.

We need to help the mass of the population discover that neoliberalism won't save it from poverty and that authoritarian socialism didn't save it either, but a democratic socialist path followed by us and the people, built by us, invented by us—this may well save all of us men and women.

Thank you.

Notes

1. Paulo joined these Paraguayan seminars for four days in September 1992. These discussions took place on September 8 in the Quinta Ykua Sati Convention Center, Asunción. The transcripts of the conversations were published under the title of *Dialoguing with Paulo Freire*, and some of these are included in this book.

2. This is *Pedagogy of Hope: A Re-Encounter with Pedagogy of the Oppressed*; see note 2, Part II, Chile.

3. Herbert Read, *Education through Art* (1943).

4. Some of Paulo's answers didn't cover all aspects of the question, or weren't transcribed in the book *Dialoguing with Paulo Freire*. Therefore we could not feature them in this book.

5. Freire is speaking here.

6. Ghettos or slums.

7. No doubt because of this interval, there was some discontinuity in Paulo's replies as he worked through the list of items. Some of these would be taken up again subsequently.

8. Campaign for democratic expression and citizenship in Paraguay.

9. Paulo is referring to the "Experience of Angicos," in Rio Grande do Norte in 1963, when he accepted European grants through the program Alliance for Progress. See Ana Maria Araújo Freire, *Paulo Freire: A Story of Life* (Indaiatuba, Brazil: Villa das Letras, 2006). This book received the Jabuti Award, 2007, second place in the category of Best Biography Book.

PART V

URUGUAY

Interviews

On Education, Politics, and Religion[1]

Neber Araujo: Professor Paulo Freire ... sixty-eight years of age ... professor at the Catholic University of São Paulo, professor at the State University of Campinas, secretary for education of the Municipality of São Paulo. He has come to Montevideo for the fifteenth anniversary of the Center for Research and Cultural Development [CIDC].

You are the author of various works in the area of education: Education as an Act of Freedom, Pedagogy of the Oppressed, The Importance of the Act of Reading, *etc. If someone saw those books in a bookshop window, he might wonder: "Is this man a pedagogue or an ideologue? Is he an educator or a politician?" Let's start with these extremes....*

Paulo Freire: Very well. ... I've got two things to say to begin with. Here's the first: when you mentioned my age, my wife, Nita—next to me here—gave me a nudge because she protects her husband and, by extension, herself. ... I'm still sixty-seven. ... She protects the three months that remain. ... Sixty-eight is an exaggeration. ...

The second thing I want to do is to congratulate you, most heartily, on the way you put this first question to me. This is the first time, in a radio or TV interview, that I have witnessed such a beautiful, such a critical introduction. ...

There is, indeed, some confusion surrounding me. Many people wonder to themselves and ask me whether I'm really a

115

pedagogue, and they often angrily affirm that rather than a pedagogue, I'm an ideologue, a politician. In suggesting this, you are adopting one of the main criticisms leveled at me by the right in my country, and you give me an opportunity to clarify this question in a few words.

What is a pedagogue? A pedagogue is a man or a woman who thinks about educational policy from a theoretical, philosophical, and critical perspective....

Sometimes he's not directly involved in educational practice, which is bad, but he's involved in the critical reflection of this educational practice. I try to do both things: to reflect on educational practice and live it, help it to evolve.

A pedagogue is therefore a technician involved in the practice of what education means, but any educational practice is, by nature, a political act ... I'm not saying that it's a party political act, but educators must make their political choices. I belong to a political party in my country, but I respect the political opinions of the students with whom I work. My activity as a teacher doesn't belong to my political party; my party has no right to influence this practice ... but what we can't deny is that educational practice is never neutral: it's enough for the educator to ask himself or herself on behalf of whom he or she is an educator, and in posing this question, he or she is preparing himself or herself to understand how it is impossible to be neutral....

Araujo: So, for you, there's no such thing as a technical pedagogue, a skeptic ...
Freire: I would say there's no one like this, not just a pedagogue. There isn't a physicist, a mathematician, a biologist, a priest, a bishop ... no one.... This thing of saying, "I'm in the world to serve the interests of humanity" is a lie.... It's pure ideology.

Araujo: So whose interests do you favor?
Freire: I favor the interests of the huge majorities of exploited people in my country.... Those are the people I'm with....

Araujo: So, for you, education should—as the titles of your books suggest—be an instrument to correct the inequalities that punish the majority of people ...

Freire: Your reference to "an instrument" was very apt. It would be totally naïve of me to say that education is "the instrument," to say that it is "the platform" for social transformation.... It isn't.... But, to an extent, it is dialectical, contradictory. Education isn't the platform for transformation, but social transformation needs education.

Araujo: Let's be quite clear: What is the difference—in your view— between education and political indoctrination?

Freire: Very well ... you seem to have been an attentive reader of my books....

Araujo: In fact, I haven't read your books ... only a few articles.... But the titles of your books are clearly provocative....

Freire: The question is fundamental for understanding my thought. All educational practice implies, in the first place, the presence of an individual known as an educator, and in the second, the presence of another individual known as a student, and in the third place, a certain content or object that mediates the two individuals. I'll give you a concrete example: in a particular course, I am the educator, there are the students, and there is an object: the critical comprehension of pedagogy. It would be my role, together with the students, to analyze this object in order to then define the specific content of the program. Educational practice also implies certain methods and techniques used by the educator, and which should, by means of the educators, facilitate an understanding of the object under analysis among the subjects involved in the process of knowledge acquisition.

Additionally, all educational practice implies certain ends, certain objects that go beyond the practice itself. This aspect, which is external to the practice but at the same time within it, is what constitutes its nature. This doesn't allow for the existence of any educational practice that is not directional: all educational practice is directed toward something.

This doesn't mean that because its practice is directional, it is therefore manipulative.... It is directional by nature, but it sometimes becomes ideologically manipulative and authoritarian. My position is the following: I live the directional nature of educational practice and I'm a democrat; I don't manipulate my students, but I don't leave them in any doubt: in the course of my work, I try hard to win over my students to my truth. This is surely my right, isn't it?

Araujo: We were talking about this concern with purity, this technical approach to pedagogy that is often sought, and this committed pedagogy that you yourself defend. You say, "When I teach I give my all, and I put forward my opinion...." In Uruguay, the banner of secularism has been flying for many decades and is a matter that is treated with great care. We defend the idea that the students should have access to all the pieces of the jigsaw puzzle and should be free to complete it for themselves.

When I listen to you, I get the impression that you provide all the pieces and give them the jigsaw already completed....
Freire: No ... I assure you I don't.... [laughter]. But your question is a good one, and a kind of trap you've laid to see if I fall in, a provocation.... What I do is to propose different positions, different hypotheses and postures to my students. Obviously, I also propose my own posture; I don't have any reason to conceal my positions from my students: they wouldn't respect me; they would think I'm ashamed to say the things for which I fight....

Araujo: You know how influential a teacher's thought and ideas are on his students ...
Freire: Yes ... and it's precisely because of this that the teacher can't hide them, and must say to his students, "I acknowledge that, from a cultural point of view, a teacher's word weighs heavily, but you must learn to measure the weight of a teacher's word. You must not listen to him or her just because he or she

is a teacher...." And in order to say all this, he or she needs to tell his or her students what he or she thinks.

The teacher isn't an alien being who fell out of the sky just like that; a teacher is a man or a woman like the students. It's the same with parents, too. No one has more influence on their children than the mother and father. For that reason, should the father conceal his religious, political, musical, or even football-team preferences from his children? When my son asks me, if I am Brazilian, "Dad, among all the international teams in the world, which one do you support?" Should I reply solemnly, "I'm not telling you so as not to influence you"? [laughter] ... That's just silly....

Araujo: But aren't these mixtures dangerous?
Freire: But is there anything in human existence that isn't dangerous?

Graziano Pascale: Some moments ago, you emphasized your right to convince, not to impose your ideas, but to convince your students. You have a long history of contact with students.... How would you sum up this period when you exercised the right to convince? What answers did you get?
Freire: Now that you have joined in the conversation, I'd like to come back to Montevideo every month to chat. This question refers to a very unique aspect of my life, of my life experience, but it isn't an easy one to answer. In the first place, because the answer is a very personal one. On the other hand, it's not easy for a man like myself, who has little sense of organization, and who doesn't keep statistics.... But I've received beautiful letters mentioning how, through conversation, through a seminar, a course, or through reading my books, without even knowing me, I've managed to exert some influence....

Some days ago, I addressed a group of teachers at Campinas about my passion for educating. Afterward, a group of young people of various ages approached me. One of them asked permission to kiss me and said, "Look, Paulo, you changed the direction of my life.... One day, in 1981, I asked you a question in the corridor of the university and you gave me an answer that caused me to change my life's path for good…."

I apologize for telling you these stories that might give the impression that I lack humility. Humility in an educator is absolutely necessary; the experience of humility influences students very deeply. An educator should be a man or a woman who can communicate humility very effectively….

I consider myself to be a happy man, not because I believe I've done a lot or achieved anything extraordinary. I'm happy because I know I did a little, but the little I did was done with passion, and I exerted influence that I consider to be fundamental from a human point of view. I am content…. In some years from now, I hope many years, I will die, but I will die satisfied….

Araujo: You are a professor at the Pontifical Catholic University of São Paulo [PUC-SP]. Does this mean that you are a Catholic, that you believe in God?
Freire: I believe in God … but PUC-SP is one of the most open institutions in Brazil. You don't have to be a Christian to work there. I have colleagues who are fine teachers and who aren't Christian, but command great respect. As a Christian, my formation is a very personal one. I'm convinced that Christians who criticize those who aren't, who criticize a film because it shows a woman's beautiful legs, who criticize someone for making love to another … these people don't believe in God. If they did believe, they wouldn't have to try so hard to make others believe…. They're people who have more fear than love. I reject this type of religiosity with all my strength….

Araujo: I'd like to go back to the beginning of this conversation, to your books, Education as an Act of Freedom, Pedagogy of the Oppressed, The Importance of the Act of Reading…. *Free yourself from what? Who is the oppressor? Free yourself from an economic, social, cultural situation … or change the whole political system?… How are we to understand this?*

Freire: It's all this that you've said, and a little bit more. What needs to be made clear is that the process of liberation is a permanent process. By this, I mean that we men and women are much more "projects," "processes," than we are completed beings. That's why I always insist that no one *is*; we are all *becoming*. But we are becoming in the midst of a reality that is also becoming, a reality that is constantly changing. We men and women, we were shaped by the contradictions of historical reality. Our ideas are forged, constituted in the material, social, historic, and cultural practice of society. This doesn't mean that because my thought is influenced by reality it can't transform the reality that has conditioned my way of thinking.

Araujo: So what are the limits and instruments for such a transformation?
Freire: In the first place, this transformation isn't the task of one person, nor that of one or two "enlightened" people. It is a social task, a task for groups of people, classes, that organize themselves for the purpose of solidarity, who gain strength at the same time that they involve themselves in a process of political transformation. I believe that this is an ethical problem, because all political problems are also ethical problems. If you were to ask me why I have committed myself so radically to this process of transformation, ever since my youth right up to the present, I would answer like this: Should I be happy in the knowledge that every day, thousands of children die of hunger in my country? Isn't this the result of a serious lack of ethics? Where is the morality of this society?

I think it's crazy that the Church tries to prohibit people from seeing a certain type of film in a society in which thousands of children die of hunger every day.... We need to hold this government accountable, to fight to destroy the structures that uphold this state of affairs. We must feel ashamed for having a good night's sleep in a society in which children, young people, and adults die of hunger. In Brazil, there are eight or nine million children of school age who have no school

... millions of adults who can't write a word.... This is a lack of ethics! So I would say that my main impulse is ethical in nature.

For me, it's no use believing in some form of transcendence and standing by waiting for Brazil to be transformed through transcendental means.... It won't work.... Transformation is a task for Brazilian men and women.... Until now, God has never put into effect agrarian reform in any country: it's men and women who should do it.

Araujo: Professor Freire, sadly our time is up. Congratulations to CIDC for its fifteen years of existence and for the invitation made to this personality, with whom it has been an honor to talk in order to agree, to disagree, and to be educated....
Freire: And for me to be educated too....

Dialogue on Education, Television, and Social Change: Interview with Sonia Breccia[2]

Sonia Breccia: Good evening. I am delighted to announce that this evening, our whole program is devoted to sharing the experience of a man who is nowadays a "living legend," as much for those who share his ideas as for those who disagree with him.

He was born sixty-seven years ago in the city of Recife, that mythical place in Brazil because of the poverty and misery that exist there, and because of the challenges it faces in the present and in the future. Over the course of these sixty-seven years, he has participated in the history of Brazilian education, but he has projected this into the future through books such as Pedagogy of the Oppressed *and* Education as an Act of Freedom, *that have been translated into a great many languages....*

He is a professor in São Paulo and also the city's secretary for education. His name is Paulo Freire, and it is him we are going to interview so that our viewers can agree or disagree with his human vision, and his understanding of education as an act of freedom. We want to reflect on television, with regard to his work as a viewer and a citizen, and with regard to ourselves who work with and produce this means of communication.

Let us therefore begin our encounter with Paulo Freire....

Freire: I was indeed born in an area that is one of the most problematic in the world. Recife is a city that has experienced a truly tragic history, with a vast, marginalized population that lives on "scraps."

It is heartbreaking to witness an "exotic" item of news in which men, women, and children look for scraps of food in certain parts of the city where rubbish is dumped.... If one of us did this, we would most certainly die within ten minutes because our bodies don't have sufficient immunity to withstand this: the body's immunity is, above all, the immunity of the social class to which the body belongs. I'm absolutely convinced of this.

Breccia: The poorer we are, the greater our immunity?

Freire: The body has a certain degree of immunity because of its need to protect itself. There is a certain measure of wisdom in nature. The question of hunger is the topic of considerable talk, much debate, and has been widely researched in Brazil: the relationship between hunger, malnutrition, and the process of learning. And there are even people who have said that hunger provokes a deterioration in a child's cognitive capacity, but this is not true.

Malnutrition obviously impairs the process of learning, but it doesn't induce in the child any more than this. This is very interesting: ten days ago, a Brazilian specialist was speaking in Campinas on how organisms that are submitted to this type of restriction manage to defend themselves; that is, the body is smaller, shorter, and as such manages to defend itself from undernourishment, from cognitive incapacitation.... Human life is mysterious....

Returning to your first question: having been born in this region and in this city, I of course witnessed at close hand the challenges of destitution. I also experienced some hunger when I was a child, even though I belonged to a middle-class family. I experienced shortages during the great depression of the 1930s. My family, a middle-class family, suffered the repercussions of this crisis and we went through times of considerable difficulty. I have mentioned this simply to underline my own experience, but I wouldn't say that I was born in any way predestined because of this.... No, not at all, because in the end, we construct ourselves socially, we are not born to *be*. My situation was an interesting one: on one hand, because of my class position, I lived alongside children who ate well, dressed well, studied, and from the point of view of the needs of the family and because of hunger, I also lived in contact with a number of children who didn't eat, didn't sleep well—in a word, children from the *favelas*.³

I was a sort of "intermediate child," a "conjunction child." I connected two social classes, without, of course, being aware of the question. But the fact that I would step out of a house where one ate well and step into a house in the *favela* where people didn't even eat led me to question why this was so. I had no answer, but I was convinced that there were many things that were wrong in my country, and my rebelliousness taught me this.

I would say that nowadays, reflecting in an adult way, the ethical question always had a profound effect on me and still does leave me deeply moved. Pay close attention to the fact that I referred to the question of ethics and not puritanism, or a philosophy of morality, because philosophies of morality horrify me, but I consider a life without ethics to be nonviable. So the ethical question was always my stimulus and I would often ask myself if it was possible that so many people should sleep well, live well, when they were surrounded by so much deprivation. Ever since my childhood I asked myself these things, I educated myself, I foreshadowed the man who, many years later, would write *Pedagogy of the Oppressed*....

So, although I could never affirm that I am, or was, absolutely predetermined by the social, cultural, economic, and ideological structures of my tragic northeastern region, I would say that, if I had been born in São Paulo, I probably wouldn't have written *Pedagogy of the Oppressed,* unless I had been born recently, because São Paulo is today experiencing a situation that is catastrophic.

Breccia: When someone thinks about the things you have said, when one thinks about those people who eat or who live on scraps, and at the same time one thinks about the favelas, *in order to make some reference to their reality, where children are born without hope of developing their capacity to think, we could ask, What has changed in all these years? How many millions of dispossessed are there in your country, how many millions of illiterates?*

Freire: Sadly, today the rate of illiteracy is increasing. If I'm not mistaken, I believe about 17 percent of Brazilian adolescents and adults are illiterate. There's something that may also explain this. Firstly, in Brazil we have eight million children of school age who don't go to school in a total population of 150 million.

That's eight million boys and girls who should be in school and aren't: the state hasn't provided them with a school. Obviously, statistics talk of eight million, but they don't tell us how they arrived at this figure; what is certain is that these children were not born into fortunate families, but are children from the working classes that are "prohibited" from attending school.

Unfortunately, I don't have figures available, but there are thousands of poor children, the children of workers, in particular in the large urban centers where the working class is organized and active, who study in the state schools. And what happens? Between the first and second year, the state school system fails thousands of these poor children, who haven't succeeded in learning to read and write. At the same time, the children who have somehow learned to read and write, and manage to progress to the fourth and fifth year, when they get to the fifth year, they begin to be failed in geography, mathematics, and history.

The result of all this is that in Brazil today, if you chart the progress of a generation that enrolls in the first grade of basic education, you'll find that only a tiny proportion completes the course in the stipulated eight years because most of those who started get expelled from school.

It's sad to see what specialists call this practice: they call it "educational truancy," as if the children had said, "Let's get out of school." ... The children don't abandon school; they are expelled from it. And this expulsion increases, year after year, the number of adolescents and adults who are illiterate.

So, in a country like Brazil, we need a political decision to be made (because this is a political and not a pedagogical problem), in order to face up to the issue of illiteracy among adults and adolescents and overcome, once and for all, the obstacles that children have to confront during their years at school.

I can talk with such assurance about this because I have been secretary for education in this vast city of São Paulo since January, and we are fighting to "change the face of school" in São Paulo, to create a different type of school, a happy school.

Breccia: I would now like to ask how this can be done and also to address another theme, which I think is one of the curses of Brazil. Please don't think I'm trying to interfere here, but for us, the problem of these street children and the violence to which they are subjected is very worrying, very painful. It's as if it were our own problem....
Freire: Before talking about the huge effort being made by a great team of highly skilled people to try to "change the face of school," I'd like to say a few words regarding a question you asked before, when you compared my childhood to today and rightly said, "Paulo Freire hasn't changed anything." ...

Breccia: I don't know whether it has changed, but the feeling one is left with is, Has it changed? Has Brazil changed?
Freire: I think you are right when you say this.... There is an initial outburst of anger, which is necessary and justified, when we ask ourselves, But has nothing changed? I would say a lot has changed.... Not the government in itself, not the decisions of the classes that rule us, that dominate us; for me, what is

changing in Brazil, and on occasion with considerable speed, is the power of decision manifested by the popular classes. They are probably far from achieving their ideal, but it is no coincidence that a party like the Workers' Party has become the party of government in thirty-six cities in the space of ten years, including São Paulo, which has a population of twelve million inhabitants.

I don't know how long it will take, and here I'm not speaking as a party activist: I speak as a man who is trying to reflect upon and understand reality. The social history of Brazil is changing, sometimes at great speed, sometimes leaving us feeling pessimistic. There are moments when the facts are so horrific that they make us wonder: has anything changed? Things are changing and I hope that this change becomes more radical and progresses toward more profound, more substantial change.

We are determined and committed to rebuilding the state school system that, during the years of the military regime, was deliberately run down by military ideology with its desire to wreck the state sector in order, essentially, to favor the private sector in its policies.

We currently have a great deal to do…. Or rather, what we've got to do now is not to discard private schools, but regain the dignity of the state school. Depending on whether the state schools go back to being what they were, the private ones will either stay or fall by the wayside; this isn't a question that worries me at the moment. What does concern me is to transform the state school into what it should be: a school that is serious in intent, worthy, a school where one teaches and learns. A school that is democratic while not merely paying lip service to democracy, that has authority without being authoritarian, and that defends liberty but does not accept licentiousness…. A school that builds, that enables children to create and to be happy within it.

This isn't easy; it's very difficult. During the first six months of our struggle, my team and I, as secretary for the Municipal Education Network in the city of São Paulo, became only too aware of how difficult it is to transform all this. The difficulty itself is a challenge to us, as is the awareness of such difficulty on the part of a large number of people. To give you and your viewers an idea, after I became secretary, I managed to organize a contribution of—so far—eighty university teachers from the State University of Campinas, the University of São Paulo, and the Pontifical Catholic University of São Paulo. They are physicists, mathematicians, biologists, sociologists, philosophers, art teachers. We've got eighty specialists working with us, looking at ways to change the school curriculum.

It's wonderful; it's a challenge that gives my life meaning and makes me want to speak with passion about what I do.

You also commented on the street children. This fills me with joy, but sadness as well.... A strange feeling between joy and sadness at having a son who is a sociologist, and who is currently in São Paulo working as a street educator (working with street children). It's a dramatic problem, and far more serious than one might imagine. Sometimes, people who are somewhat removed from the problem think the solution would be to place all these kids in a reformatory, but this would be stupid because children also go through an enriching experience on the street.

The problem is that we must change the structures of society and not the minds of these children. What is wrong isn't the child who is left in the street, but the society that allows the child to live on the streets and this is something that no one wants to see. They want to speak out against violence, against what the children do when they steal their bag, their jewels.... I'm not defending this, but I'm saying that these things exist because there's a fundamental reason for them to exist. So, at the same time that you, as an educator, have to provide a solution for this problem, you've also got to fight politically to change the structures of a society that explain why this phenomenon exists.

Breccia: I propose that in the next part of our encounter, we analyze how this transformation might take place, but from the point of view

of the media we use here, which is television. You know how successful Brazilian soap operas are in our country.... We know that in Brazil, soaps have even brought the country to a standstill, that people have even changed their work shifts; men and women.... Isn't that the case?
Freire: Yes indeed....

Breccia: The theme of this final part of our encounter with the Brazilian pedagogue, Paulo Freire, is television. Given that you were talking about these necessary changes, I assume we would not be setting you a snare by asking you to talk about this much-maligned, beloved, and feared instrument....
    How is television used in your country and how do you think it might be used? Do you like television?
    So here is the question: This instrument, television, does it have a role to play in these changes?
Freire: Firstly, I shall begin to try to answer your question, which seems a very good one to me, by saying that I seek to be a man and an educator of my time. I confess that I can't understand how an educator of this day and age can deny television, deny videos, deny computers, deny the radio, which, although now somewhat outdated, for me is still hugely important as a means of communication. I don't believe at all that television has brought the end of radio.... It's another discourse, another way of communicating, probably more human than technological, while television is more technological than human, ... which doesn't mean that it is not human as well or that it couldn't become even more so....

    To conclude my introduction, I would love to work on television; I would probably have to learn a tremendous amount because I don't know anything about it, but I would love to work on television. I am fascinated by this world of illusion, but if there is a world of illusion that is profoundly real, then this is it....

Breccia: How come?
Freire: You can have a background like this one [in the studio] that gives the impression of a wood, but it's merely the

suggestion of a wood, and invites the viewer to re-create and to play with his or her imagination. Your background, through the use of imagination, touches the real. There is a close relationship between the imaginary and the real, the concrete.…

On the other hand, for this type of work to use television we need to be aware that there is no such thing as neutral television. A means of communication like this is unavoidably, and eminently, political and ideological; what can well happen is that the person working on television, for example, the young cameraman, knows the crucial role he plays with the camera while few people are aware of this in their homes, because he and those who work with the image he sends the viewers can select the image they prefer—for example, my hands are portrayed in this manner.… This conveys a certain meaning, has a certain impact, or maybe it doesn't have one at all.… So, a man like the cameraman, while I am talking, can extract from me the possibility of another message conveyed. If he doesn't agree with my ideological and political positions, if I become distracted and place myself in a position in which I might appear ridiculous, he can zoom in on my eventual ridiculousness. He can do what he wants with me … but of course he can also do wonderful things that enhance my ability to communicate.… Apart from this, the owner of the television channel has a political and ideological choice, and he won't agree to work against his own political sympathies just because he likes my eyes or my beard. If I were to work in Montevideo, I probably wouldn't get four [television] programs like yours [given my ideology]. Not because of you, but because of the political-ideological forces that lie behind the television, behind the cameras. This needs to be said so that the people know that there's no innocence in this activity, but what seems fundamental to me is that it's not enough for me to refuse to give an interview … or to dislike television.

Breccia: Following your line of argument, it seems to me that there are two important points. You are sufficiently confident in this form of media, in the intelligence of people and in your own capacity to communicate to know that, even as we speak (we're talking hypothetically), beyond any private-sector interests (remember we're on a state TV channel), beyond this camera that, as you pointed out, may serve these interests, beyond the interviewer who may eventually serve these interests, there is an interviewee and a popular intelligence that may surpass all these factors.

Freire: I believe they do exist, and I will bet on it, as an educator and as a political being. This is part of my life, I can't deny it, but on the other hand, I've got to learn to be better in my lifetime, and it won't be possible to be better or more efficient in my lifetime if I deny the value of television.

My dream, for example, is that a time will come when society will have been so transformed and humanized, a society that some may say is utopia, and in which I will say "Yes, it's a utopia...." But wretched are the men and women who don't dream.... And my dream is that one day television will treat the people with decency.... You know I'm deeply irritated by people who work for the television news service in a "scientific," neutral way. Sometimes, they don't seem to know what they're doing. They assemble a whole stack of news items from all over the world and then "pulverize" them. By this I mean that sometimes we have to listen, in the same breath, to a news item about some woman somewhere who has won a beauty contest, followed by a news item about China.... They leave China and talk about a flood.... What happens is that millions of viewers watching the news don't have time to look critically in order to at least understand one of these items, because they switch from one topic to another so quickly that no one can understand anything. This isn't a coincidence, nor is it a question of incompetence on the part of those putting together the news. This is the ideological and political know-how of the dominant class, and it happens throughout the world, and not just Brazil....

Breccia: See, Mr. Freire, how this leads us nicely to the next president of your country ... and we don't know who it will be. When I was in Brazil last February, Brizola headed the polls; that is, the process was just beginning and the campaign hadn't yet begun, but he had 18 percent of people's preferences, with Lula not far behind.

At that time, there was a name that wasn't widely known, although over the last two months we have heard it mentioned a lot: Fernando Collor de Mello, a young man of forty who has been governor of Alagoas, who has resigned from the government and now has 42 percent, while Brizola only has 11 percent and Lula 8 percent.

All this may change, but you can see that I'm steering the argument into your terrain. The family of Collor de Mello is very powerful, very wealthy, and, apart from this, the proprietor of many television channels, and one of the things international commentators have observed in your country is the extraordinary hold Collor has on communication. . . .

Freire: Of course, I agree with you, but for me there's an even deeper point, but which doesn't take anything away from your observation, and it is this: Collor is conducting a moralistic campaign in Brazil, given that, for some years now (above all ever since the military governments, but before that as well), the country has been undergoing an interesting albeit tragic phase, which is something that I call "the democratization of dishonesty."

It really is quite extreme. No one believes in anyone; a person's word has lost any shred of dignity. A man holding a position of responsibility in public life says something on television today, and the viewers at home say, "Tomorrow, the opposite is going to happen. . . ."

Breccia: There's no trust. . . .
Freire: No . . . ! It doesn't exist. And a country experiencing this listens to Collor's promise to put an end to this and that . . . it wants to believe him . . . then it ends up not believing him. Now, I have no right to say Collor is lying. What I want to say is that the Brazilian masses, experiencing this contradiction, are now insisting upon honesty, a certain degree of ethics without which one can't do politics. It's a demand being leveled at politicians, their leaders. Now, what [Collor] says, propagated through a form of media such as this, television, explains, as

far as I can see, Collor's position. My impression—and this is the impression of a supporter of Lula because I'm a member of the Workers' Party—my conviction is that this situation may change, it must change, but in order for it to change, we need to work closely with the people and we need to devise new channels of communication with the popular masses.... This is an extraordinary means of communication.... Television is an extraordinary means of communication, but we need to teach people, we need to learn to view it from a critical standpoint.

I confess that I'm sometimes shocked to meet pedagogues, scientists, who fear and even reject television. I just cannot understand this, because I would be naïve if I thought television was a neutral instrument, that it was completely "well behaved."... I know it isn't, but we can't pass up the opportunity to have it as a means of communication at the service of a process of humanization.

Breccia: To finish, I would be grateful, Professor Freire, if you would allow me to summarize as follows: concluding what you have just said, I would like to ask you about the power of this means of communication that you have given us an insight into, and with which we might agree or disagree, but which we need to consider. Do you think this power is total, to such an extent that it makes people less free and "sells" us the candidate or the formula that they want us to buy?
Freire: No, it's not quite like that.... I believe its power is undeniable and beyond dispute, but not as powerful as we thought. There has even been research carried out in the United States showing that a certain overkill in commercials leads people to adopt an opposite position.

Now, as far as I'm concerned, we cannot deny the importance of this means of communication. Far from it: for me, what is fundamental is that we should fight politically for it to become more ethical, that it should better serve those who are exploited, dominated, and in order for this to happen, we need to change society itself, and in changing society, the ethical and political question we are proposing is not to perpetuate, via this form of communication, a taste for self-preservation, a taste for the status quo. That is, in a different type of society, we should charge this form of media with the responsibility of making society different: more dynamic, more creative.

Breccia: Paulo Freire, I'd like to thank you for appearing on Hoy por hoy *during your stay in Montevideo....*
Freire: My thanks to you and to your television channel for inviting me. I am very happy because it's the first time I've been in Montevideo, and today alone, I've had two delightful interviews: one this morning on Radio Sarandí, and the other with you this afternoon. Many thanks....

Breccia: To you, and all our viewers ... "Hoy por hoy."...

That's all for today. I am sure you've all been able to reflect upon the themes we have discussed: polemical, debatable, loved by some, resisted by others, but always necessary....

And so, we bring today's encounter to a close....

Notes

1. Interview conducted by Neber Araujo and Graziano Pascale for the program *En Vivo y en directo* (*Live and Direct*), broadcast by Radio Sarandí, Montevideo, on June 22, 1989.
2. Interview conducted on June 22, 1989, on Channel 5, Uruguay, for the television program *Hoy por hoy* (*Nowadays*).
3. Ghettos or slums.

Index

academia, 4, 18, 96–97, 102–103
academic knowledge, 102–103
accountability, 121–122
aesthetics, 21, 47, 64, 70
agrarian reform, 13
alternative society, model for,
    77–80
animal communication, 61
apathy, 25
Araujo, Neber, 115–122
Araújo Freire, Ana Maria "Nita,"
    46, 111, 115
Argentina, 13
Arias, Germán, 3
art, 81–82
assistencialism, 98–99
authoritarian education, 60, 63,
    64–65
authoritarianism, 21, 47–48, 69
autonomy, 98, 103–108
autosuggestion, 98–99
awareness, 38

Barbosa, Ana Mae, 82
Being More, 7–8
Bezama, Boris, 43–49
bourgeoisie, 23
Brazil, 104–105; academia in,
    96–97; changes in, 126–128;
    dictatorship in, 96; education
    in, 31, 125–128; fatalism in,

13, 35; poverty in, 123–126;
    presidential elections, 131–133
Breccia, Sonia, 122–134

capitalism, 68, 77
Catholic Church, 97, 121
CEBs. See Ecclesiastical Base
    Communities (CEBs)
Center for Research and Cultural
    Development (CIDC), 115
change, 22, 27
Chauí, Marilena, 73
Chiapas, Mexico, 27
children: curiosity of, 19; in
    poverty, 123–126; street, 128.
    See also students
Chile, 43–44
CIDC. See Center for Research and
    Cultural Development (CIDC)
citizenship, 36
class struggle, 36–37
cognoscible objects, 18–20
coherence, 24, 27, 28, 44, 80, 81,
    90–91
Collor de Mello, Fernando, 78–79,
    84, 106, 109, 132
common sense, 30, 85
communication, 11, 34–35, 61, 133
communism, 77
comprehension, 11
conceptions, 21

About the Author

The late Paulo Freire was a world renowned educator, writer, and social activist. His belief that educators, administrators, researchers, and families have transformative power has made his work valuable beyond the educational field. His intimate and critical work with and for populations affected by poverty and economic, social, and political oppression has made him one of the most recognized scholars of education as a means for social change and liberation of oppressed peoples. Freire is considered the most important educator of the last fifty years of the twentieth century.

Freire's early book, *Pedagogy of the Oppressed*, sold more than 1 million copies and was translated into fifty languages. His book *Pedagogy of Freedom* (1998) expands and elucidates his theory of a more communicative and dialogic method that leads to a greater awareness of consciousness. Freire labeled this process *conscientization*, which, according to him, implies "learning how important the obvious becomes as the object of our critical reflection, and by looking deeply into it, I have discovered that the obvious is not always as obvious as it appears." The central educational objective of conscientization is to awaken in the oppressed the knowledge, creativity, and constant critical reflexive capacities necessary for the oppressed to demystify and understand the power relations responsible for their marginalization and, through this recognition, begin a project of liberation.

Among the books translated from Portuguese by Paradigm Publishers are *Pedagogy of Indignation* (2004) and *Daring to Dream* (2007).

CPSIA information can be obtained
at www.ICGtesting.com
Printed in the USA
LVHW010023200620
658570LV00011B/1305